THE TRAMWAYS OF BRIGHTON

AND ITS SURROUNDS

by David Voice

Published by Adam Gordon

ALSO BY DAVID VOICE

How to Go Tram and Tramway Modelling
London's Tramways Their History and How to Model Them
What Colour Was That Tram?
Tramway Modelling in 'OO' Gauge
More Tramway Modelling in 'OO' Gauge
The Illustrated History of Kidderminster and Stourport Electric Tramway (with Melvyn Thompson)
How to Go Tram and Tramway Modelling, 2nd Edition
The Millennium Guide to Trams in the British Isles
The Definitive Guide to Trams in the British Isles
Toy and Model Trams of the World, Volume 1: Toys, Die Casts and Souvenirs (with Gottfried Kuře)
Toy and Model Trams of the World, Volume 2: Plastic, White Metal and Brass Models and Kits (with Gottfried Kuře)
Next Stop Seaton! (with David Jay), 4 editions
How to Go Tram and Tramway Modelling, 3rd edition
Hospital Tramways and Railways, 1st and 2nd editions
Freight on Street Tramways in the British Isles
British Tramcar Manufacturers, British Westinghouse and Metropolitan-Vickers
Works Tramcars of the British Isles
The Age of the Horse Tram
Monorails of the World
Tram and Bus Tokens of the British Isles
Battery Trams of the British Isles
Mono-Rail, The History of the industrial monorails made by Road Machines Ltd, Metalair Ltd, and Rail Machines Ltd
Tramway Reflections
Shocking Solutions to a Current Problem
Seaton Tramway—Its Electric
Seaton Tramway—The Valentine's Day Storm
The History of Worcester's Tramways
Last Rides—Funeral Trams Around the World
All Dressed Up and Somewhere to Go, the History of Decorated Tramcars in the British Isles
Slot Machines, The History of Cable Hauled Street Tramways in the British Isles
Kidderminster and Stourport Electric Tramway Company Ltd.
Explosive Power on Tramways in the British Isles
Tramways of the Potteries

The Author

David Voice has been interested in trams, both full size and model, for as long as he can remember. David is the author of many books about tramways and tram modelling; he has also been published extensively in the model railway press. David has recently retired as the Small Scale Modelling Adviser to the Tramway and Light Railway Society, a role he held for over 40 years.

A catalogue entry for this book is available from the British Library
ISBN 978-1-910654-25-5
Publication no. 129

Published in 2020 by Adam Gordon, Kintradwell Farmhouse, Brora, Sutherland KW9 6LU
Tel: 01408 622660

Printed by 4edge, 22 Eldon Way Industrial Estate, Hockley, Essex, SS5 4AD.

Production by Barnabas Gordon

THE TRAMWAYS OF BRIGHTON AND ITS SURROUNDS

CONTENTS

"PERSEVERANCE"

A contemporary cartoon of Magnus Volk published in the "Brightonian" on 17 November 1883 titled "Perseverance".

INTRODUCTION

When I started researching information for this book I was surprised how fascinating the tramways in the Brighton area were and how flexibly the term tramway was used. Although today the legal definition of a tramway is far more confined, I have taken the earlier broad use of the word. All the forms of transport included in this book, bar one, were in their time called tramways. The exception to this rule is the proposal to build a monorail along the sea front. This is included because of the potential impact it would have on the Volk's tramway, the oldest operating electric railway in the world. Other, now no longer with us, transport systems have their own unique characteristics. Probably foremost among them is the unique "Pioneer" the only sea-going tramcar ever built. Another amazing system was the Glynde Telpherage Tramway, an electric monorail that ingeniously used the single support rail as a positive and negative electrical supply. Even the more orthodox Corporation Tramway was dominated by the absence of any cooperation between the local Authorities that prevented their residents from enjoying a cohesive public transport service.

Where I have used photographs taken by others, I have acknowledged the source in its description. All photographs that do not have a credit were either taken by myself or are from my personal collection of historic images and to save space do not have an individual credit.

ACKNOWLEDGEMENTS

It would not have been possible to write this book without the very generous help I received from many people and organisations who have considerable knowledge of the various systems. In every case they have generously shared information and guided me to further resources. Without all this help the book would be smaller and less informative. I owe a great debt of gratitude to each and every one.

Gerry Cork, John Fox, Ian Gledhill, John Godgard, R. Knight, Barrie McFarlane, Roger Monk, Stuart Strong, Peter Williams, Brighton Tram 53 Society, Volk's Electric Railway Association and Volk's Electric Railway

I would also want to thank Adam Gordon for his invaluable advice and guidance for this book and the many years that he has been publishing my books. I am indebted to him.

PHOTOGRAPHS

Top left:	Brighton Trams
Top right:	A Brighton and Shoreham tram body sold after the closure of the horse tramway.
Bottom left:	Volk's Electric Railway
Bottom right:	Brighton and Rottingdean Seashore Electric Tramroad.

CHAPTER 1

BRIGHTON DISTRICT TRAMWAYS 1884 - 1888

The only known photograph of a Brighton District Tramways steam tram and trailer. The gentleman standing in the centre of the side of the trailer is John Blaker, the Managing Director.

The Sussex village of Brighthelmstone led an unremarkable life until 1841 when the London and Brighton Railway opened. This enabled Londoners to have day trips or longer holidays by the seaside. It is located in a 'U' shaped valley in the side of the South Downs, which prevented any extensive building development to the north or the east. To the west were the separate communities of Hove and Shoreham and in the 19th and early 20th centuries there was a high degree of rivalry between the three towns. As tramways developed in Britain, the Brighton area attracted speculators who proposed as many as six separate Bills to Parliament for the establishment of horse tramways connecting the three communities. The first attempt to build a tramway in Brighton came in 1872 when a Bill was promoted for a line from Kemp Town along the promenade to Southwick Harbour, a total of 8¼ miles. There was strong opposition and the Bill failed. Clearly Brighton Council were not impressed by proposals to lay tram lines in their Borough. Indeed, resistance from the Councils of Brighton and Hove saw all subsequent Bills promoted prior to 1900 fail, bar one. The one that was successful was The Brighton District Tramways Company Act of 1882 and this was successful only because it proposed a route entirely within Shoreham-on-Sea, hence preventing any objections from Brighton or Hove Councils.

The successful application to lay tram rails in the street was made by the Brighton District Tramways Company with the agreement of Shoreham Council. The Company obtained authorisation in 1882 to lay 5¼ miles of 3ft 6in gauge track from Western Road, passing Shoreham Station, along Ham Road, Lower Brighton Road, Albion Street, Wellington Road, Boundary Road, turning right into New Church Road, terminating at the Hove boundary by Upper Westbourne Villas. The track was single

An enlargement showing more detail of the Wilkinson locomotive, number 2 in the fleet.

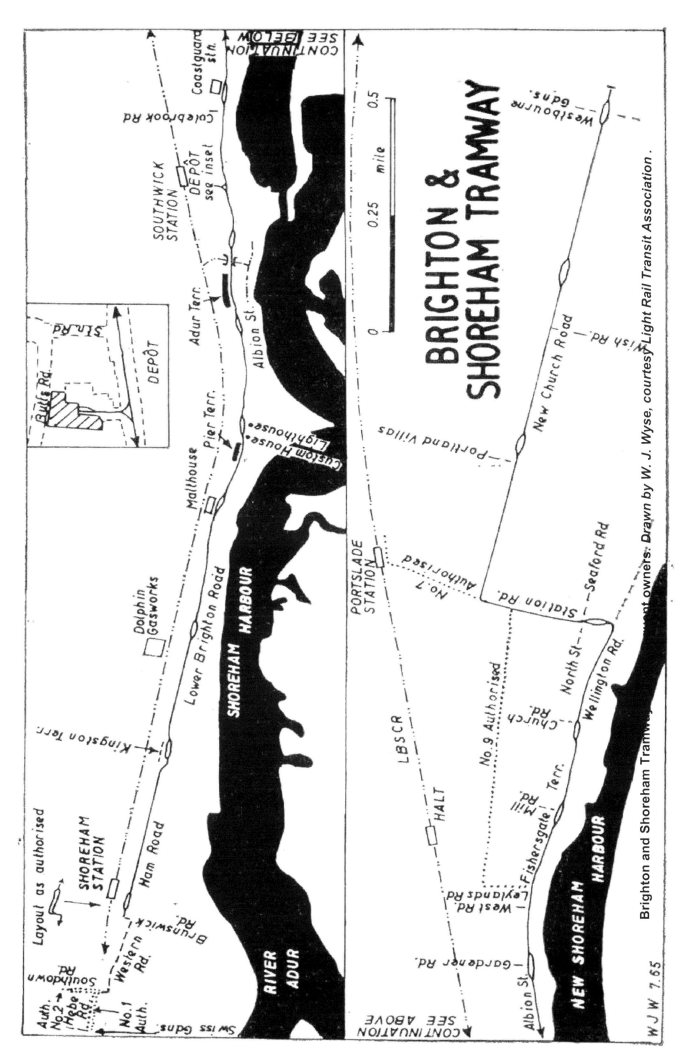

BRIGHTON & SHOREHAM TRAMWAY

Brighton and Shoreham Tramway

W J W 7.65

with fifteen passing loops. The Company was authorised to use steam traction on all the route, except the western end beyond Shoreham Station (from the Burrell Hotel to Swiss Gardens), where the Board of Trade Inspector only allowed horse power to be used due to the narrow roads and very sharp bend from Brunswick Road into Western Road. Initially this short section of the Tramway was operated by horse power, hauling the steam trailers. When the horse tramcars were purchased one was used to operate this short section of the Tramway. However, this short section of the line proved uneconomic and after a short while it was abandoned. The sharp curve from Ham Road into Brunswick Road was to cause problems during steam operation, as when the steam trams terminated outside Shoreham Station the locomotives had to turn into Brunswick Road in order to clear the loop and run around their trailer. Due to the sharp curve the locomotives had an unfortunate habit of derailing. At the other end of the line many passengers wanted to travel all the way to the centre of Brighton, so the Company arranged for a horse omnibus connection to meet the tramcars at Upper Westbourne Villas. This was route 112 operated by the Brighton and Preston United Omnibus Company.

The 1882 Act authorised 5 miles 2 furlongs 6 chains and 20 links of tramways to be built as follows:

Tramway No. 1: 6 chains, 40 links in length, situated in the Parish of New Shoreham, from a point in Hebe Road 5 chains east of Victoria Road and proceeding in an easterly direction to a junction with Tramway No. 2 at a point in Southdown Road 1 chain north of the northern parapet of the L.B.S.C. Ry. Bridge over Southdown Road. The line to be double track throughout.

Tramway No. 2: 4 furlongs 6 chains and 40 links situated in the Parish of New Shoreham, commencing in the Southdown Road at a point 2.5 chains

north of the junction with Tramway No. 1 and proceeding in a southerly direction along Southdown Road, thence in an easterly direction along Western Road, thence in a northerly direction along Brunswick Road and thence in an easterly direction along Ham Road and terminating at the junction with Ham Road and Lower Shoreham Road. To be single line except from a point 0.5 chain from its commencement for a distance of 2.5 chains to the south and from a point in Brunswick Road 1.2 chains north of

Like many Victorian tramways, the Brighton District Tramways had a terminus outside a public house that would also double as a tramway passenger shelter.

Western Road for a distance of 3 chains to the south and from a point in Brunswick Road 1.2 chains north of Western Road for a distance of 3 chains along Ham Road to the east.

Tramways Nos. 3 to 6 inclusive: 2 miles 4 furlongs 7 chains of single line to be laid along the coast road from the end of Tramway No. 2 to Station Road, Portslade, 3.5 chains south of the south-east corner of Red House farmhouse.

Tramway No 7: 2 furlongs 4 chains and 50 links situated part in the Parish of Portslade and part in the Parish of Aldrington, commencing with a junction with Tramway 6 and proceeding northwards in Station Road to a point 1.5 chains south of the south gate of the level crossing at Portslade Station then easterly along a new road to be constructed in the Parish of Aldrington to a point 4 chains east of Station Road. To be single line except for 3 chains northward from a point 5 chains northward from its commencement and for 4 chains westward from the terminal point in the new road.

Tramway No. 8: 1 mile 9 chains, partly in the Parish of Portslade and partly in the Parish of Aldrington, commencing at a junction with Tramway No. 7, at a point 3.75 chains north of the south-east angle of Red House farmhouse in Station Road and proceeding eastwards along New Church Road and terminating at a point 4.5 chains east of Westbourne Villas. To be single track with passing loops situated as later described. This part of the tramway was in Hove and this became an issue later in its life.

Tramway No. 9: 5 furlongs 3 chains and 45 links, situated partly in the Parish of Southwick and partly in the Parish of Portslade and commencing by a junction with Tramway No. 4 in Fishersgate Terrace at a point 0.2 chains west of Leylands Road and proceeding along Leylands Road and an intended extension thereof in a northerly direction for a distance of 6 chains or thereabouts, then in an easterly direction along a new road to be formed on certain lands in the Parishes, crossing Church Road, Portslade at a point 0.1 chain north of the southern boundary wall of St. Andrew's Church ground and proceeding eastwards to a point in Station Road 3.4 chains south of the south-east corner of Red House Farmhouse, there to make a junction with Tramway No. 6. To be single line except in the new road from a point 6.3 chains from the commencement for a distance of 3 chains eastward.

Not all these lines were actually built. Tramways No. 1 and No. 9 were not constructed and part of Tramway No. 2 was not built. The gauge of the Tramway was to be 3ft 6in and the speed of the tramcars was not to exceed 8 mph. The Company was authorised to raise £40,000 in capital using 4,000 shares of £10 each. It could also borrow up to £10,000. The Company was given two years to construct the Tramway and work it with animal, steam or other mechanical power. The Company was required to run workmen's tramcars Monday to Saturday inclusive, two before 7 a.m. and two after 6 p.m. The fares were limited to a sum not exceeding ½d per mile (but the Tramway could charge a minimum of ½d).

The Tramway Company contracted Messrs Winby of Westminster to build the Tramway. Work commenced in August 1883 and it made use of the harbour at Shoreham by bringing in most of the building materials by sea. At the same time as the work started the Tramway Company put forward an application to extend the Tramway towards Brighton by laying lines in Hove. However, the Hove Council were anti-tram and despite some public support the Council continued to oppose any tramway in its area. This opposition may not have been purely bloody mindedness as some roads were very narrow and one bottleneck meant that two horse omnibuses were unable to pass each other. A tramway track would have been a considerable obstacle.

Outside the Burrell Hotel, Shoreham, passengers new to the area would get an unwelcome surprise when they found that the Hove destination was the Corporation boundary, still some distance from the town centre.

Children of the town gather in the yard of the tramway depot (note the tramcar behind them) preparing for a parade to celebrate St George's Day.

Work on laying the tramway started in 1883 with a single track line that had 15 passing loops. The section along Station Street and the blind right angle turn into New Church Road was single track, and appears to have been problematic for drivers who entered the section without being able to see if any other tramcar was already occupying it. The first test runs were carried out on 19th June 1884. Major-General Hutchinson, from the Board of Trade, carried out an inspection on 27th June and public services began on 3rd July, with two Wilkinson steam tram locomotives and two Falcon trailers. Local dignitaries were invited to the formal opening ceremony, which was followed by the customary lunch and speeches. One speaker, presumably a Director, stated that "in a very short time the trams would be carried not only through Brighton and Hove but to Newhaven to the east and Arundel in the west". One of the guests at the opening was Mr Wilkinson, Managing Director of the steam tram locomotive Company. In his speech he commented that "horses shied a bit at the engines at present, but they would get 'educated up' to them very quickly." This optimism was rather deflated a month later when four horses pulling a coach on its way to Brighton became frightened by a steam tram engine and they bolted, overturning the coach. Four passengers were thrown off the coach, three of whom escaped serious injury, but the fourth was trapped between the coach and the tram and was seriously injured. This accident had worried the Shoreham Council, as they had not realised that the tramway was to be powered by steam. They sought legal advice to force the Tramway Company to only use horse power, but now that the Company had the Act empowering them to use steam power, there was little the Council could do. To add to the Company's concerns, the townspeople disliked the steam locomotives and there were many complaints about the noise, smoke and oil emitted by the engines.

In 1884 the Tramway Company presented their Bye-Laws and regulations to the Board of Trade for ratification. These included "No passenger shall, while travelling in or upon any carriage, play or perform upon any musical instrument." Another interesting regulation was "No person other than a passenger or intending passenger shall enter or mount any carriage, and no person shall mount or hold on by or to any part of any carriage, or travel therein, otherwise than on a seat provided for passengers." This was followed by three more regulations each prohibiting more passengers than available seats. Then rule 20 must have been reassuring to all passengers, "No person shall travel in or on any carriage of the Company with loaded firearms.", which begs the question "What about unloaded firearms?" The Bye-Laws came into force on 19th November 1884.

Encouraged by the opening of the Tramway, the Company promoted two extension Bills in 1884 and another in 1885 to lay tramways in Hove. However, once again opposition from the local Council meant that they failed to pass through Parliament. Traffic receipts were much lower than had been anticipated and the Tramway was losing money. In an attempt to lower costs, three single deck horse trams were ordered from the Oldbury Carriage and Wagon Company and these entered service on 23rd May 1885. Each was hauled by a single horse. The local paper, the Brighton Herald, reported that the horse drawn tramcars were to replace the steam locomotives. However, things may not have been as clear cut as the report suggests, as the Company continued running the steam trams and also ordered a third steam tram locomotive in 1885 from John Fowler of Leeds, with a further two ordered. When the first was delivered it was soon recognised that it was not suitable for service on the Tramway. The engine was returned to Fowler and the order for the other two was cancelled. The horse trams were authorised to operate over the short distance between Shoreham Station and Southdown Road. But this part of the system was found to be uneconomic and it was later abandoned, the new terminus becoming the Burrell Hotel, near the station building. Just a month after the new tramcars were delivered there was a serious accident when horses hauling a tramcar bolted, and were involved in a collision that damaged the tram.

In 1883 there was another tramway proposal, this time from the Brighton and South Coast Tramways to lay a 3ft 6in gauge tramway from the Aquarium, Brighton, to the High Street, Newhaven, taking the coast road east of Brighton. This seems to have been a speculative venture that failed to attract sufficient backing, as a new application was made in 1884 for a similar tramway. However, nothing further was heard of the scheme.

The life of the Company was disrupted when, in November 1885, a Mr Evan Hare petitioned for the Brighton District Tramways Company to be wound up. Mr Hare of Hare and Company, Solicitors, was described as a shareholder. The matter was heard by the High Court of Justice and the decision was made on 5th March 1887 that the Company be wound up. The Court appointed a Liquidator to take over the management of the Tramway on 16th May 1887.

In 1886 a further seven double deck horse tramcars were obtained from the Oldbury Carriage and Wagon Company. But all was not well and the Company was haemorrhaging money. The Tramway paralleled the coastal railway and those wanting to travel further afield than Shoreham would choose the railway. To add to the troubles there were reports of steam trams having had a frequent habit of derailing. The Directors sought a cheaper form of motive power and experiments were undertaken using the Elieson battery system. Chaimsonovitz Prosper Elieson had set up the Electric Traction Syndicate to promote his invention of a battery tram locomotive. Records are not entirely clear, but it appears that

A tramcar waits outside the Burrell Hotel for its departure time. It looks like a cold day from the absence of passengers on the upper deck and the extra clothing worn by the driver.

one of the Tramway's horse tramcars (believed to be number 10) and converted it to battery operation by fitting an electric motor and placing 80 boxes of accumulators (weighing 1 ton 5 cwt) beneath the seats. The first demonstration took place on 27th July 1887 which was disappointing. The single axle drive did not generate sufficient power and the tramcar stopped frequently and the demonstration was restricted to the line close to the depot. The tram

As the section of the line from Shoreham Station to Southdown Road was continuing to lose money the Liquidator decided to close it. This made one of the horse tramcars redundant and it was sold to the Rhondda Valley and Pontypridd Tramways Company for £45. The Liquidator recognised that the most used part of the line was from the centre of Portslade to Upper Westbourne Villas and some of the single deck cars provided an additional short

It is not known if it was by intent or accident that car number 4 was involved in the parade to celebrate the Golden jubilee of Queen Victoria on 20th June 1887.

was modified by fitting a chain drive linking the axles, making it into a four-wheel drive vehicle. This was an improvement and it was able to complete the 4½ mile journey at an average speed of 11½ mph (a top speed of 20 mph was claimed, though it was restricted to a speed of 6mph). It was also reported that the Electric Traction Syndicate demonstrated a battery locomotive hauling one of the steam trailers. While Elieson was able to sell a battery tramcar to the Dunedin Tramway in Australia, the Brighton Company did not purchase one, possibly this was due to the precarious financial situation of the Tramway Company. Instead, they ordered two extra horse tramcars from the Oldbury Railway Carriage & Wagon Company Limited, this time both were double deck cars. Tramcar number 10 had the batteries and motors removed and reverted to horse power. In 1887 an Aveling and Porter steam tram locomotive was purchased and was the last steam locomotive to be obtained by the Tramway. Alas, it was only in service for less than two years.

working service over just this section. A new Company, the Brighton and District Tramways Company Limited, was formed that took over the ownership of the Tramway.

In 1921, some eight years after the closure of the tramway, Henry Cheal, Honorary Curator and Librarian to the Sussex Archæological Society, wrote "The Story of Shoreham". The history included reference to the Tramway, as follows. "Trams formerly ran between Shoreham and Hove. The rails were laid and it was opened in the early 'eighties, the cars being drawn by steam-engines. They ran from the Hove Borough boundary, by way of New Church Road, through Portslade, Southwick and Kingston, thence along Ham Road and Western Road to Southdown Road. We have said ran, but it is probable that no self-respecting traction engine ever "snailed" it like the Shoreham steam tram. Moreover, it had a decided propensity for running off the line at every possible opportunity, and few were the occasions when it

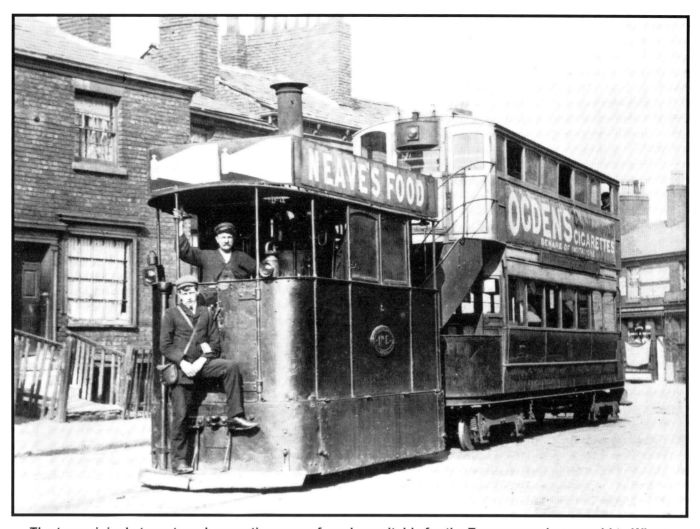

The two original steam tram locomotives were found unsuitable for the Tramway and were sold to Wigan District Tramways in 1889 and this was renumbered 5 (the other became 6).

kept to the rails in turning "Pennifold's Corner," in its painful endeavour to get into Western Road.

The journey was afterwards curtailed to terminate at the end of Ham Road, and eventually, the engines being so unsatisfactory, horses took their place. These cars ceased running about eight years ago and the rails have since been removed."

FLEET

Steam tram locomotives.

1884 No 1 Wilkinson 0-4-0 withdrawn 1889
1884 No 2 Wilkinson 0-4-0 withdrawn 1889
1885 No 3 (i) Fowler 0-4-2 withdrawn 1885*
1887 No 3 (ii) Aveling and Porter 0-4-0 withdrawn 1889

Steam trailers

1884 Nos 1 & 2 Falcon double deck bogie car withdrawn 1889
1885 Nos 3 & 4 Falcon double deck bogie car withdrawn 1889

Horse tramcars

1885 Nos 1 - 3 Oldbury Railway Carriage & Wagon Co. Ltd. single deck
1886 Nos. 4 - 10 Oldbury Railway Carriage & Wagon Co. Ltd. double deck

Battery tramcar

1887 No 10 was converted to battery operation, but rebuilt back to horse power later the same year.

LIVERY

Locomotives: dark brown
Tramcars: light brown and cream

NOTES

* A further two tram locomotives were ordered from Fowler, but the order was withdrawn when locomotive No 3 had to be returned to them as unsuitable for the Tramway.

CHAPTER 2

BRIGHTON AND DISTRICT TRAMWAYS COMPANY LIMITED
1888 - 1889

Diminutive tramcar number 1 hardly has enough room on its side for the name of its new owners.

The new Company took over the operation of the tramway in 1888 and continued running it in a similar way to the previous Company. However, the situation did not get any easier and the actions of the new owners were not sufficient to keep the Company financially solvent. Within a year it too failed and went bankrupt in May 1889. The Court appointed Henry Spain of London as Official Liquidator on 28th March 1889 to manage the Tramway. The Tramway was once more put up for sale. It is unclear what happened to the Tramway at this time. The Company employees may have continued the operation under the management of the Liquidator, or the services may have ceased while the future was being determined. However, it is known that at this time the steam trams and one trailer were sold off to Wigan and Worcester respectively. The Liquidator sold the remaining enterprise on 6th November 1889 to "The Brighton and Shoreham Tramway Company" (actually a Company based in Leicester that had been incorporated on 30th October 1889) for the sum of £10,000.

FLEET

Steam tram locomotives.

1884 No 1 Wilkinson 0-4-0 withdrawn 1889
1884 No 2 Wilkinson 0-4-0 withdrawn 1889
1887 No 3(ii) Aveling and Porter 0-4-0 withdrawn 1889

Steam trailers

1884 Nos 1 & 2 Falcon double deck bogie car withdrawn 1889
1885 Nos 3 & 4 Falcon double deck bogie car withdrawn 1889

Horse tramcars

1885 Nos. 1 - 3 Oldbury Railway Carriage & Wagon Co. Ltd. single deck
1886 Nos. 4 - 10 Oldbury Railway Carriage & Wagon Co. Ltd. double deck

LIVERY

Locomotives: dark brown
Tramcars: light brown and cream

CHAPTER 3

BRIGHTON AND SHOREHAM TRAMWAYS COMPANY LIMITED
1889 - 1898

Tramcar number 4 has its new owners painted on the rocker panel.

The Liquidator was once again in charge of the Tramway and to recoup some funds he sold items of the rolling stock to other tramways. The two Wilkinson steam tram locomotives were sold to Wigan Tramways, one of the double deck horse tramcars was sold to the Worcester Tramway and the horses were sold to local merchants. This leads to the speculation that he was unsure if he could sell the rest of the concern. In fact, the Brighton and Shoreham Tramways Company purchased the Tramway in

Tramcar number 5 on a bright summer's day.

In the late 1800s youngsters left school at a far younger age than today. Tramway Companies took advantage of this (young lads earned far less than adults) to employ boys as conductors. It was considered to be a very good job and there was much competition for any vacancy.

November 1889, albeit with a skeleton fleet. The tramcars that were sold with the Tramway were three single deck horse cars and one double deck horse car. The new Company started a limited service as soon as they acquired the Tramway. The Board of Trade authorised the Tramway to raise £10,000 through stocks (£8,890 were issued). Immediately £7,790 was spent on improving the line and buying horses and new tramcars. In 1891 five new double deck horse tramcars were purchased.

From this point the Tramway appears to have settled down to a relatively comfortable existence. For the remaining years of ownership, it gave a regular, if unexciting, profit to its shareholders and quietly continued to give service to the people of Shoreham. The development of the Tramway is illustrated by the expansion of the number of horses from 29 in 1890 to 35 in 1898. The most exciting event for the Tramway was in 1898 when the British Electric Traction Company purchased a controlling interest in the system and became the owners on 27th June 1898.

FLEET

Horse Tramcars

1885 Nos 1 - 3 Oldbury Railway Carriage & Wagon
    Co. Ltd. single deck
1886 No. 4 Oldbury Railway Carriage & Wagon Co.
    Ltd. double deck
1891 Nos 5(ii) – 9(ii) Unknown, double deck

LIVERY

Yellow and cream

The western terminus was close to Shoreham Station.

CHAPTER 4

BRITISH ELECTRIC TRACTION COMPANY LIMITED
1898 - 1903

It is believed that this photograph was taken soon after the British Electric Traction Company acquired the Tramway. All the staff are wearing smart new uniforms.

In the 1890s the British Electric Traction Company (BET) was starting to develop an empire of street tramways. The British Electric Traction (Pioneer) Company was set up in 1895 when there were just 50 miles of electric tramways in Britain. The aim was to acquire horse tramway systems and convert them to electric operation. The Shoreham Tramway caught the interest of the Company and on 27th June 1898 the BET acquired the Tramway. The plan of the BET was to electrify the operation and to extend the line east to Seven Dials in Brighton and west as far as Littlehampton, creating an American style interurban. One of the first moves by the new owners was to issue drivers and conductors with uniforms, reflecting the professional approach of the Company. The BET then entered into negotiations with the adjacent Local Authorities for the conversion of the Tramway to electric operation and for its expansion. At this time Brighton was exploring the possibility of building its own electric tramway, while Hove Corporation was resistant to having any tramways within its area and blocked any move to lay tramway lines. The result was that the BET had to make the best of the horse tramway by improving the services. An early decision was to increase the fleet of tramcars by purchasing three additional double deck cars that arrived in 1900. The fleet then consisted of eight double deck horse tramcars and three single deck horse tramcars.

Under the highly professional management of the BET, the early days of the Tramway showed a profit of around £1,000 per annum. When the Brighton Corporation Electric Tramways opened in 1901 the BET saw an opportunity to try again, this time proposing to link their system with the new Corporation Tramway. However, this would mean getting agreement with Hove Council to run trams in their streets. To add to the problems, the report of the accounts for the year 1901 complained that the income from fares was being badly affected by serious competition from the Portslade to Hove omnibus service. There was no dividend payment that year.

In 1903 the BET applied to the Board of Trade for authority to extend their Shoreham Tramway to Worthing in the west and Hove and Brighton in the east, having running rights over the new electric tramways of Brighton, under the Hove, Worthing and District Tramways Bill. The BET were seeking powers to build and operate a coastal tramway from Littlehampton to Hove to connect with the Brighton system. In 1904, anticipating getting authorisation to convert to electric operation and to expand the system beyond Shoreham, the BET formally took control of the Tramway and set up a new Company, Hove and Worthing Electric Tramways, Limited to develop the Tramway. The most noticeable immediate change for the public was the tramcars were repainted in BET red and cream with the BET magnet and wheel emblem. Unfortunately, the attitude of Hove had not changed and again they opposed the idea of tramways running in their streets and countered by announcing plans to open their own

Parliament alleging that the BET were not compliant with Standing Orders. The Council also applied for and obtained their own Bill, proposing to build their tramway to connect with the BET system. However, it was never constructed. The next initiative was an approach by the Company to the Hove and Portslade Corporations to see if they were interested in purchasing the Tramway. They expressed an interest and offered £1,584 (comprising £1,122 from Hove and £462 from Portslade). This was far too low for the BET, who referred the issue to arbitration. The arbiters recommended a price of £4,673,

Repainted in the BET red and cream livery and sporting the magnet and wheel logo, this tramcar looks very smart.

electric tramway that would run from Shoreham Station, over the route of the Brighton and Shoreham Tramway, continuing across Hove to connect with the Brighton Corporation Tramway. Hove applied for and obtained an Act authorising them to lay tramways in their Borough. This effectively blocked any application from others and it transpired that this was its purpose, as Hove had no intention of actually building a tramway. At this time the Tramway discovered that their returns to the Board of Trade were incorrect. The length of the system continued to be recorded at 4⅓ miles long. It appears that no one adjusted this when the short section of line from Shoreham Station to Southdown Road was closed, reducing the system to 4⅛ miles.

Rebuffed by Hove again, the BET looked in the other direction to Worthing, but got a similar response from the Worthing Council who said that they had plans for their own municipal tramway. The BET responded with their own Bill to extend their Tramway to the Shoreham boundary to connect with the Worthing system. The Worthing Council petitioned

which was unacceptable to the Councils and the deal failed. From this time, it appears that the BET lost interest in the Tramway, having no possibility of converting the line to electric operation or of extending it.

Things only got worse, as in June 1905 the Worthing Motor Omnibus Company opened a bus route along the coast from Worthing to Hove, extended to Kemp Town, east of Brighton, in October. It has been said that the bus drivers would jam stones in the grooves of the tramway track in order to derail the tramcars, though this was unlikely. The BET central management, having taken control and unable to expand the system, decided in 1907 that their only option was to close the Brighton and Shoreham Tramway.

To add to the woes there was a serious incident on 17th May 1908 when tramcar number 12 was involved in an accident that injured five people. With serious bus competition, the Company decided to withdraw most of the services, just running the bare legal minimum to prevent the Council from closing

The BET had hoped to extend the tramway and convert it to electric operation. However, they were thwarted by Hove Corporation and competition from omnibuses reduced the number of passengers.

it down. The three single deck cars were withdrawn from service, while cars 10 – 12 were rebuilt to single deck, though due to their size each still required two horses to pull them. The drastically reduced service continued for two years and was not improved until 10th June 1910 with a regular, if diminished, service. The Tramway continued to operate until 1911 when Hove Council introduced a Bill to operate trolleybus services in their area. The Bill included provisions allowing the Council to remove the Tramway rails in the area. Once the Council had their Act ratified they lost no time in removing the Tramway rails along New Church Road, between Portslade Station and Westbourne Gardens. According to reports at the time the rails were lifted so rapidly that the road surface was left in an appalling state. The omnibus Companies running along the road complained to the Council and were allowed to reintroduce horse buses that were not so damaged. It was a year before the Council re-laid the surface of the road. The BET had lost a quarter of their system. Unable to extend in either direction and with just a part of their original Tramway the BET decided to cut their losses and close the system. But before they did the Tramway got a publicity boost for an unexpected reason. Albert James, a local boy, had obtained a job as conductor on the Tramway (probably the sole conductor). He was interviewed by the "Daily Mail" and hailed as the youngest conductor in England. The article appeared in the paper on 12th May 1913. By this time the service had been reduced to just one tramcar, number 10. Even that had been modified and was reduced to single deck, keeping staffing costs to a minimum.

However, the whole purpose of the BET was to build new electric tramways or convert existing horse tramways to electric operation. . It was not part of their remit to keep running horse tramways, particularly one running at a loss. So the system was doomed to stop operating and this finally occurred on 6th June 1913.

The caption on the photograph is "The last tram from Shoreham to Hove", the consequence of Hove Corporation obtaining an Act allowing them to remove the tram rails in their area.

Tramcar number 10 decorated for the last day of operation.

Tramcar number 10, probably the only tram in service, was chosen to undertake the final passenger run. Albert James was the conductor and a wreath was attached to the tramcar to indicate the closing of the system. The remaining track was raised and sold for scrap, while two of the tramcars were sold privately to become sports pavilions on Shoreham Beach. Thus the horse Tramway ceased operating, no doubt much to the relief of the BET.

FLEET

Horse tramcars

1885 Nos. 1 - 3 Oldbury Railway Carriage & Wagon Co. Ltd. single deck.
1886 Nos. 4 - 10 Oldbury Railway Carriage & Wagon Co. Ltd. double deck, scrapped by 1899.
1891 Nos. 5(ii) – 9(ii) Unknown, double deck.
1900 Nos. 10(ii) – 12 Unknown, double deck, later rebuilt as single deck.

LIVERY

BET red and cream

The last journey of the Tramway with a crowd of local people acknowledging the demise of their Tramway.

CHAPTER 5

BRIGHTON CORPORATION TRAMWAYS
1901 - 1939

Tramcar number 1 has been decorated ready for the opening ceremony of the Tramway.

Under the 1870 Tramways Act either Local Authorities or private Companies could build tramways, after obtaining the appropriate Act of Parliament, but only private Companies were allowed to operate tramways. The reasoning being that roads were open to the public and anyone could take their wheeled vehicles onto the road. Since the tramway tracks were in the road, Parliamentary logic was that the same principles should be used. In operation it was impractical for such a free-for-all operation. Nearly all tramways were operated by a single user, or by special arrangements to ensure there were no conflicts. Local Authorities drew the attention of Parliament to what they felt was an anomaly. In 1896 the Government introduced an amendment allowing Local Authorities to operate tramways. Many took advantage of this by either building their own tramways or by compulsorily purchasing existing tramways after 21 years from their opening.

Brighton attracted speculators with plans to build and operate street tramways. The first proposal was the Brighton Street Tramway Bill in 1872. The promotors recognised the difficulties of the town, with its steep hills and narrow streets. Their idea was to lay lines along the sea front with links to the main railway stations in Brighton and Hove and a branch to the barracks at Preston. It was also planned to lay a line to the yard of the Brighton old Gas Light and Coke Company in Kemp Town. The promotors saw potential for delivering fuel and other materials to the gas works. The Parliamentary Committee rejected the Bill because of objections to the lines along the promenade as the roads were too narrow. As this was a key feature of the proposals the promotors withdrew their interest. Things lay quiet for some years and it was not until 1883 that Magnus Volk laid his Tramway line along the beach. This is described in more detail later in the book. In 1884 the Brighton District Company made an application with the Brighton District Tramways Extension Bill, as described in chapter 1. Later in the year another application was presented, this time by the Brighton and South Coast Tramways Bill. This proposed a line starting at Kemp Town Railway Station in the east of Brighton. The line would go from the station, south to the coast road then eastwards along the coast road (now the A259) passing by Rottingdean, Saltdean and Peacehaven to terminate in the centre of Newhaven. Both Bills were abandoned, but the Brighton District Tramways Extension Bill was resurrected in 1885. However, it did not fare well when presented at the Parliamentary Committee stage. Brighton Corporation opposed the scheme, the map provided by the promotors was in parts unreadable and the roads on the map were described as being wider than they actually were. As a result, the Bill was withdrawn.

The development of electric tramcars made running routes over hilly roads, like those of Brighton practical. The modification to the 1870 Act allowing public bodies to operate tramways provided an attractive opportunity to Brighton Corporation. In the autumn of 1886 the Corporation debated the issue and decided to make moves to build and operate an electric tramway in the town. At the Corporation meeting on 10th November 1898 it was agreed to prepare a Parliamentary Bill to obtain the necessary authority. The first move was to set up a Tramways Committee that examined which roads should have a tram service. They decided a fact finding trip was required and on 21st April 1899 the Tramways Committee took a trip to Boulogne, Rouen, Paris, Brussels, Glasgow, Leeds, Sheffield, Halifax and Blackburn. The result of the tour was a report that recommended that the new Tramway should be powered by electricity using an overhead wire power supply. The Committee also considered which routes should be operated, having decided to avoid as much as possible the existing routes served by the Brighton, Hove and Preston United Omnibus Company. London Road was also omitted as it was an existing route of Ballards horse buses. However, this was questioned and it was decided to put a tram route along London Road. The Corporation hired Joseph Kinkaid as Advising Engineer and he expressed concerns at the narrowness of Lower Dyke Road. The Corporation went ahead only to find that Parliament would not authorise a route along Lower Dyke Road, instead it said that the route should turn from Dyke Road into New England Road at Seven Dials and cross London Road at Viaduct Road. There was one other major problem. The Corporation had planned to acquire Longhurst's Brewery, partially to widen the road, but also to build their tram depot. However, a fizzy drinks manufacturer had just bought the factory and did not want to relinquish it, although they were willing to lose part of the land in order that the road could be widened. The manufacturer suggested an alternative location for the tram depot, while the Corporation suggested that the manufacturer moved into other premises. It was left to Parliament to reach a decision. It sided for the manufacturer and instructed the Corporation to find an alternative location.

The details of the proposed routes were:

Tramway No. 1: commencing in Montpelier-road at or about the point at which the north-eastern side of Western-road intersects it, proceeding thence in a northerly direction along Montpelier-road, Denmark-terrace and Vernon-terrace to, and terminating at or about the junction of Vernon-terrace with Dyke-road.

Tramway No. 2: commencing in North-street at a point 32 yards or thereabouts northwards of its junction with Western-road, passing thence northward along North-street, into and along part of Upper North-street and Dyke-road and terminating at or about the junction of Dyke-road with Vernon-terrace.

Tramway No. 3: commencing by a junction with Tramway No. 2 at or about the junction of Dyke-road with Vernon-terrace and thence in a northerly direction along Dyke-road and terminating at a point 143 yards or thereabouts southward of the point at which the boundary between the parishes of Preston and Patcham crosses said road.

Laying track in Lewes Road at the junction with Elm Grove.

22

Tramway No. 4: commencing by a junction with Tramway No. 1 at or about its termination, as hereinbefore described, passing thence in a north-easterly direction into and along   Chatham-place and New England-road and terminating in London-road, at or about the junction of Viaduct-road and London-road.

Tramway No. 5: Commencing in London-road by a junction with Tramway No. 4 at or about its termination as above described passing thence in an easterly direction into and along Viaduct-road and terminating in Brunswick-place or Ditchling-terrace at or about a point opposite the north side of Rose Hill-terrace.

Tramway No. 6: commencing in London-road by a junction with Tramway No. 5 at or about the junction of London-road with Viaduct-road, passing thence in a northerly direction into and along Beaconsfield-road and Beaconsfield-villas, into and in an easterly direction along the Drove into and terminating in Ditchling-road at a point 28 yards or thereabouts southward of the junction of Hollingbury-road with Ditchling-road.

Tramway No. 7: commencing by a junction with Tramway No. 6 at or about its point of termination hereinbefore described, passing thence in a southwardly direction along Ditchling-road, into and terminating in Brunswick-place or Ditchling-terrace at a point 20 yards or thereabouts northward of the junction of Kingsbury-street with Brunswick-place.

Tramway No. 8: commencing by a junction with Tramway No. 7 at or about its point of termination as hereinbefore described, passing thence along Brunswick-place part of Waterloo-place and Richmond-place, and terminating in Richmond Place at a point 177 yards or thereabouts northwards of the junction Richmond-street with Grand-parade.

Tramway No. 9: commencing in Richmond-place by a junction with Tramway No. 8 at or about its point of termination as hereinbefore described, passing thence southward into and along St. Georges-place, Gloucester-place, Marlborough-place to and eastward along part of Church-street, and northward along Grand-parade and Richmond-place, terminating at a junction with Tramway No. 8 at or about its point of termination hereinbefore described.

Tramway No. 10: Commencing in Brunswick-place or Ditchling-terrace by a junction with Tramway No. 8 at a point 20 yards or thereabouts northward of the junction of Kingsbury-street with Brunswick-place, passing thence in an easterly direction into and along Union-road to and terminating in Hanover-place by a junction with Tramway No. 11, hereinafter described, at a point 19 yards or thereabouts northward of the junction of Union-road with Hanover-place.

Tramway No. 10A: Commencing by a junction with Tramway No. 8 in Brunswick-place or Ditchling-terrace at or about the junction therewith of Francis-street, passing thence northward and eastward into Union-road, and there terminating by a junction with Tramway No. 10 at a point 34 yards or thereabouts eastward of the junction of Rose-hill with Union-road.

Tramway No. 11: in the parishes of Brighton and Preston in the borough of Brighton commencing in Richmond-place by a junction with Tramway No. 8 hereinbefore described, at or about the northern end of Richmond-place, passing thence in a north-easterly direction into and along Waterloo-place, Richmond-terrace, Hanover-crescent, Hanover-place and Lewes-road and terminating in that road at a point 223 yards south-westward of the point at which the Boundary of the Borough crosses the road.

Tramway No. 12: commencing in Hanover-place by a junction with Tramway No. 11 and proceeding up Elm-grove, terminating at a point 35 yards or thereabouts south-westward of the junction of Elm-grove with Lewes-road, passing thence into and in an easterly direction along Elm-grove and terminating opposite the easternmost corner of the premises occupied by Brighton Workhouse in that road.

Tramway No. 13: Commencing in Elm-grove by a junction with Tramway No. 12 at a point 20 yards or thereabouts eastward of the junction of Queens Park-road with Elm-grove, passing thence in a south-westerly direction into and along Queens Park-road, Egremont-place and Upper Rock-gardens, terminating at or about the southwest end of Upper Rock-gardens.

Before the Act was passed Tramways Nos. 1, 2 and 3 were removed from the Bill. Later in 1903 a further Bill was promoted that included Tramway No. 3. With these amendments the Act received Royal Assent on 30th July 1900. The Act gave the Corporation five years in which to build the Tramway. Building and operating the Tramway would be challenging as it had very steep sections, indeed only the Halifax Tramway had a steeper section of track. For example, the Elm Grove route climbed 400 feet in just half a mile.

In anticipation of the Act being passed the Corporation had appointed Thomas Bradley Holliday as Tramway Engineer on 15th June 1900. He recommended that the Tramway should operate on a 550 volts system and be built to the narrow gauge of 3ft 6in, but application should be made for agreement for the tramcars to be the normal 6ft 6in wide (narrow gauge cars were usually restricted to 5ft wide). Advertisements were published inviting tenders for laying the track, erecting overhead and for the initial 30 tramcars. The track laying contract was won by Macartney McElroy of Bristol; Bolckow,

Track being laid in The Steine during the 1904 extension of the tramway to the Aquarium.

Vaughan and Company of Middlesbrough supplied the rails and the Tramway ordered 30 tramcars, the bodies being constructed by George F. Milnes of Birkenhead. Unusually Brighton chose to place the tram headlights on the upper deck end panels rather than the dashes.

Despite the ruling of Parliament, in March the Corporation negotiated the purchase of the Longhurst's Brewery from the fizzy drinks manufacturer (no doubt paying more than if they had been able to compulsorily purchase the building). However, it was found that the land was marshy and would not be able to support the weight of the tramcars. The Corporation looked around again and selected two adjacent sites in Lewes Road. Existing buildings were demolished and work started on the depot. The first tramcar was ready for delivery in May 1901. The Tramway Manager went to the factory to inspect the cars, which were found satisfactory. The management chose a livery of burgundy and cream, that over the years faded to dark brown and cream.

At this point the Tramway had some misfortunes. Contractors were late in the delivery of materials, due to difficulties they had in getting supplies, which significantly delayed the construction. Despite the opening being later, the management went ahead with recruiting staff. Experienced motormen. conductors and inspectors were attracted from other tramways around the country, while local people were employed for maintenance and track-work jobs. The initial 30 tramcars were built by Milnes for delivery in 1901/2.

The Lewes Road route (designated 'L' as Brighton did not use numbers for their routes, rather a letter taken from the destinations) the depot was on the route and so trams were on their route when leaving it. The first test run was carried out on 26th September 1901 and the Board of Trade Inspectors arrived in November 1901. They boarded car 23 and had a three-hour tour, stopping to give the track and points a detailed examination. The Inspectors were pleased with what they saw and the certificate to open the route was issued on 19th November, with an official opening ceremony taking place on 25th November 1901. Seven highly cleaned and polished tramcars were decorated with flags and bunting and stood waiting at the Victoria Gardens terminus for the official party. The Mayor of Brighton and Councillors were accompanied by senior members of the Tramway management who boarded the tramcars for a trip along Lewes Road. The first tram left just after midday driven by the Mayor (under close supervision of the driver!). On the way back the party stopped at the depot for a quick tour of inspection. Returning to the tramcars they proceeded back to Victoria Gardens where the Mayor formally declared the tramway open. On that first afternoon and evening the tramway carried 19,074 paying passengers.

Work on the remaining routes was carried on as quickly as possible. Route C opened on 28th December. Route B opened on 8th January 1902, quickly followed by route D on 23rd January. With the expansion of the tramway more tramcars were needed and an order for 10 more trams from Milnes had been scheduled for delivery in 1903. In March

1903 the Brighton Herald newspaper printed an article detailing the receipts for the tramway. It had been calculated that in order for the Tramway to pay for itself an income of £700 per week was required. Initially the numbers of the public using the Tramway meant the target was reached. However, the novelty of the Tramway soon wore away and the numbers of passengers and receipts started to fall. The Herald reported that by the end of March receipts had fallen and were some £70 per week short of the sum necessary to meet the running costs. However, the newspaper was optimistic and anticipated that the situation would be improved when more holiday makers arrived for the Bank Holiday. Also there were still some routes yet to open.

The Tramway ordered another ten tramcars from the United Electric Company for delivery in 1904/5 completing the orders for the initial fleet. The last two planned routes, N and S, were opened on 26th June and 27th July 1904, completing the Tramway system. However, a further route was added in July 1905, route T, a round tour over several of the routes, giving passengers the opportunity to see much of Brighton and having 15 minute stops at the Race Course and Tivoli Crescent. Many of the routes terminated at Victoria Gardens. The track layout meant that all the tramcars took an anticlockwise route around the Gardens. This saved the tramcars having to have their trolley poles turned and the driver having to change ends. Instead, they could be driven around the loop and carry on with their return journey. Like many electric tramways, Brighton was authorised to generate their own power, which could also be sold to the general public. A generating station was built at Southwick with a substation in North Road. 1902 also saw the appointment of a new Engineer, Herman Volk, son of Magnus Volk, builder of the seafront electric railway.

Having completed all the tramways authorised under the 1901 Act Brighton promptly applied for another Bill for extensions to the system. These were:

Tramway No. 1: Commencing in Church-street by a junction with the existing tramway at a point 1.80 chains eastward of the north entrance to The Royal Pavilion and passing along Grand-parade and Pavilion-parade, thence around the Old Steine and terminating in Pavilion-parade at a point 1.50 chains north of the northern end of the northernmost of the Old Steine enclosures. Length 3 furlongs and 4 chains (of which 2.70 chains were to be double track and 2 furlongs and 1.30 chains single track).

Tramway No. 1A: Commencing in Grand-parade by a junction with the existing tramways at a point 1.50 chains northward of the junction of Church-street with Grand-parade and terminating in Grand-parade by a junction with Tramway No. 1 at a point 2.50 chains northward of the north side of Edward-street. Length 2 chains of single track.

Looking very smart, tramcar number 1 leads the parade on opening day. *Author's collection.*

25

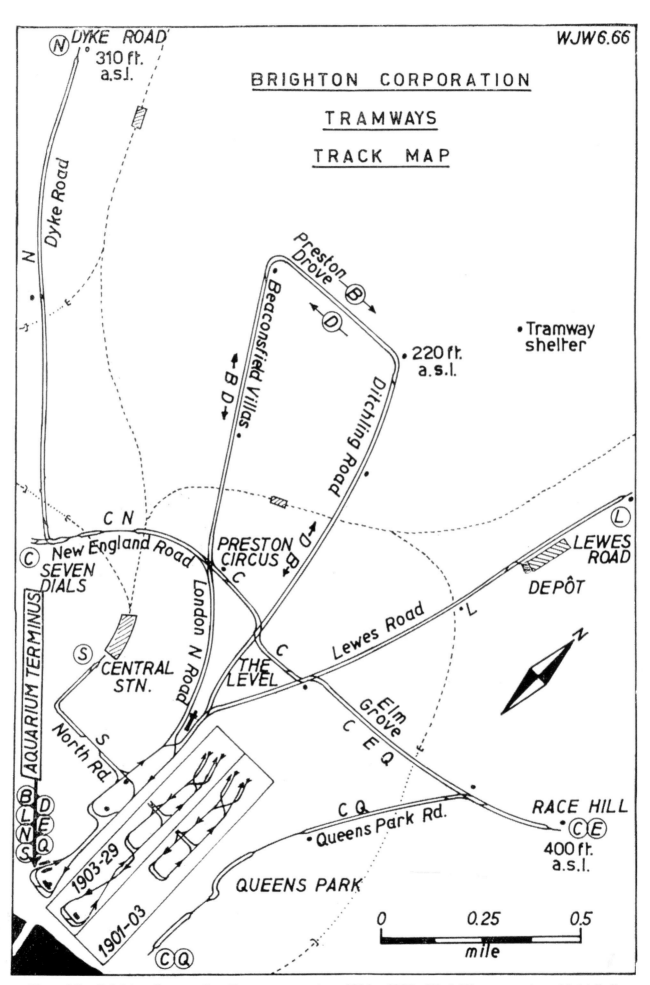

Map of the Brighton Corporation Tramways system 1901—1939. *W. J. Wyse, courtesy Light Rail Transit Association..*

Number 11, one of the first batch of tramcars to enter service, on the Dyke Road to Tivoli Crescent route.

Tramway No. 2: Commencing in Beaconsfield-road by a junction with the existing tramway therein at a point 1.50 chains north of the junction of Viaduct-road and Beaconsfield-road, thence in a southerly direction into and along London-road, York-place and St. Georges-place into and terminating in Gloucester-place by a junction with the existing tramway at a point 0.50 chain south of the south side of Gloucester-street. Length 4 furlongs and 2.00 chains (of which 3 furlongs and 6.80 chains were to be double track and 5.20 chains single track).

Tramway No. 2A: Commencing in New England-road by a junction with the existing tramway at a point 1.50 chains east of the north-east side of Elder-place and passing thence into and in a southerly direction along London-road and terminating by a junction with Tramway No. 2 at a point 2.5 chains south of the junction of New England-road and London-road. Length 3.00 chains of double track.

Tramway No. 2B: Commencing in St. Georges-place by a junction with Tramway No. 2 at a point 1.00 chain southward of the south side of Trafalgar-street and thence southward into and along Rich-mond-place and into and terminating in Grand-parade at a point opposite Richmond-street. Length 4.30 chains of single track.

The London-road line opened in 1903 with the re-maining routes opening a year later in 1904. The Corporation applied for another Act (the Brighton Corporation Act 1903) to build further lines to com-plete the system:

Tramway No. 1: Commencing in Dyke-road at a point 1.00 chain northwest of the junction of Dyke-road with Goldsmith-road, thence passing along Dyke-road and terminating in Dyke-road at a point 4.50 chains southward of the point at which the boundary between the parish of Preston and Patcham crosses Dyke-road. Length 1 mile, 1 fur-long and 6.40 chains (of which 1 chain was to be single track and 1 mile, 1 furlong and 5.40 chains double track).

Tramway No. 1A: Commencing in Chatham-place by a junction with the existing tramway at a point 1.00 chain northeast of the junction of Chatham-place with Prestonville-road and terminating in Dyke-road by a junction with Tramway No. 1 at its com-mencement. Length 1.90 chains of double track.

Tramway No. 2: Commencing in Buckingham-place by a junction with Tramway No. 4 at a point 1.00 chain east of the junction of Buckingham-place with Chatham-place and thence along Goldsmith-road, terminating at a point at which the boundary be-tween the parishes of Brighton and Hove crosses Goldsmith-road. Length 1 furlong, 1.03 chains of double track.

Tramway No. 3: Commencing in Grand-parade by a junction with the existing tramway therein at a point 0.70 chain southward of the northern end of the southernmost enclosure of Victoria-gardens and proceeding thence along North-road and Queens-road and terminating at a point in Queens-road 0.40 chain south of the main entrance gates to the Lon-don, Brighton and South Coast Railway Station.

Length 3 furlongs, 8.50 chains (of which 9.20 chains were to be of single track and 2 furlongs and 9.30 chains double track).

Tramway No. 3A: Commencing in the road between the northern and southern enclosures of Victoria-gardens by a junction with Tramway No. 3 at a point 1.00 chain west of the junction of the said road with Grand-parade and terminating by a junction with the existing tramway therein at a point 1 chain north of the junction of the said road with Grand-parade. Length 1.50 chains of single track.

Tramway No. 3B: Commencing in Gloucester-place by a junction with the existing tramway therein at a point 2.00 chains northward of the junction of Gloucester-place with the road between the north and south enclosures of Victoria-gardens and terminating in Marlborough-place by a junction with the existing Tramway No. 3 at a point 0.50 chain east of the junction of North-road with Marlborough-place. Length 2.60 chains of single track.

Tramway No. 3C: Commencing in North-road by a junction with Tramway No. 3 at a point 2.00 chains east of the junction of Cheltenham-place with North-road and terminating in Marlborough-place by a junction with the existing Tramway therein at a point 2.50 chains south of the junction of North-road with Marlborough-place. Length 3.00 chains of single track.

Tramway No. 4: Commencing in Terminus-road at a point 1.00 chain north of the junction of Guildford-road with Terminus-road and terminating in Dyke-road by a junction with Tramway No. 1 at its commencement. Length 2 furlongs, 9.05 chains of which 1.00 chain was to be single track and 2 furlongs, 8.05 chains of double track.

The Act placed restrictions on the Tramway. Tramway No. 4 was not to be built until it was possible to connect it with Tramway No. 3C. This was impossible immediately as the Corporation was unable to purchase existing property that blocked the building of Tramway No. 3C. In fact, the Corporation was never able to purchase the required property and so this line was never built.

Initially most tramway routes used the one-way system around Victoria Gardens as one terminus. However, in 1903 the turning arrangements were revised and a new loop built from the Old Steine loop, taking the Tramway past the Royal Pavilion and close to the Aquarium. Services over the new loop started on 7th November.

As the system expanded with new routes opening the Corporation needed more tramcars and it was planned to purchase a further 20 in 1903. The Tramway invited tenders for the new cars. The specification required trucks of "Peckham style of construction" or "Brill type". The lowest tender (£9,770) was from the Brush Company that quoted using Brush trucks. Another tender was submitted by the Dick, Kerr Company for £10,200 and clearly Dick, Kerr complained as the Tramway announced that the Brush Company's tender was out of order and required them to produce a new quote using Brill trucks. The Brush Company did change their quote to use Brill trucks, however, the price rose to £10,210. The result was that the Tramway Committee announced it was recommending the Corporation accept the quote from the Dick, Kerr Company.

The first car 18 was part of the original fleet and in its later years was illuminated with coloured electric lights. Here it waits at the Aquarium terminus.

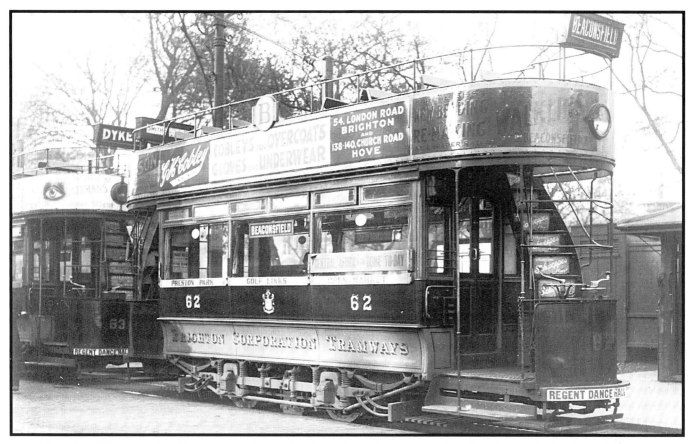

Number 62 on route B to Beaconsfield Road waiting at the Aquarium terminus. *Author's collection.*

The Brush Company decided to draw the attention of the public to this decision, stating that it was an injustice that British Manufacturers were debarred from competing for the supply of trucks. This resulted in an emergency meeting of the Tramways Committee. No decision was reached and the Brush Company held a meeting of their workers to put their side of the story. These meetings were extensively reported in the national and local newspapers. This resulted in a special meeting of the Tramways Committee that resolved to ask the Corporation for permission to withdraw the recommendation to give the Dick, Kerr Company the contract. However, no decision was reached and the matter appears to have been referred back to the Tramways Committee.

Further meetings of the Tramways Committee were held but a decision on the matter continued to be delayed. In the meantime, the Brush Company published letters of support they had received. The General Manager of Sheffield Corporation Tramways, Mr A. L. C. Fell and the General Manager of the Underground Electric Railway, Mr Jas. R. Chapman had both written to support the quality of trucks made in Britain. The situation clearly caused the Corporation to seek a compromise and the final solution was to split the order into two separate orders of ten cars each. The first order for ten cars numbers 31 – 40 was placed with the United Electric Company with Brush A type trucks. A further ten tramcars were ordered in 1904 from Dick, Kerr Company, numbers 41 – 50 (numbers 41 – 46 were delivered in 1904 and 47 – 50 in 1905). These had Brill 21E trucks, which were to become the standard

truck for all subsequent tramcars.

The move to the UEC as supplier was possibly prompted by unfortunate experiences with the first tramcars. It was found that they required far more maintenance than expected. It appeared that the timber used for the bodies was inferior and the tramcars soon required substantial maintenance. There was also trouble with the Peckham trucks breaking axles and it was found that they were underpowered for the steep Brighton hills. The Brill 21E trucks were more powerful than the other makes of truck on the other cars. This provoked a new problem as they were able to climb the hills better than the other makes, consequently tending to catch up with the tram in front of them, causing a bunching of the service. The response of the Tramway was to place all the new cars on the Lewis Road route on faster timing than the other cars. Eventually all the earlier tramcars were given Brill 21E trucks and more powerful motors.

Initially there was a turning loop at Victoria Gardens, which meant that the trams turned some distance from the coast line. This was inconvenient for the holiday makers heading for the pier and beach. The Corporation rectified this in 1903 by extending the tramway to the Aquarium with a new turning loop. The Victoria Gardens loop was anticlockwise. On leaving Victoria Gardens for the new Aquarium loop there were two crossovers, so that the trams also went around the new loop in an anti-clockwise direction, which kept the tramcars' loading platforms on

29

Car number 9 at the railway station terminus, with plenty of people shopping or travelling.

platforms on the inside of the loop, keeping the flow of joining and leaving passengers away from the other road traffic.

The final section of the Tramway system was the short line from Victoria Gardens along North Road then turning north to terminate at the railway station.

On race days every available tram was pressed into service. This shows the long queue of trams waiting outside the race course for the day's events to finish, when hundreds of spectators would board them.

This route was opened to the public on 27th July 1904. This year also saw a tragic incident. A car was stopped on Elm Grove and when the driver started moving off the wheels spun and the tram slid back down the hill. The conductor told the passengers to stay on the tramcar, but two ladies were very frightened and jumped from the tramcar. Unfortunately, this action led to their deaths. The tramcar derailed at the junction with Lewes Road, but stayed upright. All those who stayed on the tramcar escaped with no injuries.

At this time there was a move by passengers to persuade the Corporation to introduce transfer tickets enabling passengers to make a journey using two routes, but only pay a single fare. The matter had been passed to Mr Holliday, the Tramway Manager. He presented a report to the Tramways Committee pointing out that there was a universal one penny fare on the Tramway and to introduce transfer tickets would reduce receipts and would complicate the role of conductors. The Tramway Committee adopted the report and rejected the proposal to use transfer tickets.

1904 also saw the Tramway taken to the High Court when Messrs Macartney, McElroy and Company sued it for payment for work they had carried out in building the Tramway. The argument was about the payment for foundations for the tram track. The builders claimed that this work was an extra to the contract while the Tramway argued that it was included in the overall contract. The Judge was highly critical of the Corporation's Engineer and Surveyor and the Town Clerk. His decision was that the Company be awarded the £14,000 they claimed plus costs, subject to final decisions regarding the exact amount. The Company wrote to the Corporation offering settlement in receipt of £12,000 plus costs.

Having laid all the tramways authorised under the initial Act, the Corporation's thoughts turned to adding new routes. The first to be explored was one along Preston Road to near Preston Park Railway Station. Unfortunately, the opposition party in the Corporation were not inclined to support the application. In order for the motion to be adopted at least ⅔ of the Councillors needed to participate in the vote. Although the vote was 26 for the motion and 3 against, the total number of Councillors voting did not reach the required ⅔ of all Councillors, due to abstentions. Thus the proposal was defeated and a tramway was never built along Preston Road.

The Tramway had an unexpected setback in 1905 when Thomas Holliday, the tramway General Manager and Engineer, resigned to take up a similar post for the Hastings Tramway Company. The blow was made worse because he took with him 41 of the men from the Brighton Tramway, a significant proportion of the workforce. On 1st May the Tramway promoted William Marsh from Assistant to full

Car number 4 was decorated to celebrate the Coronation of King George V in 1911.

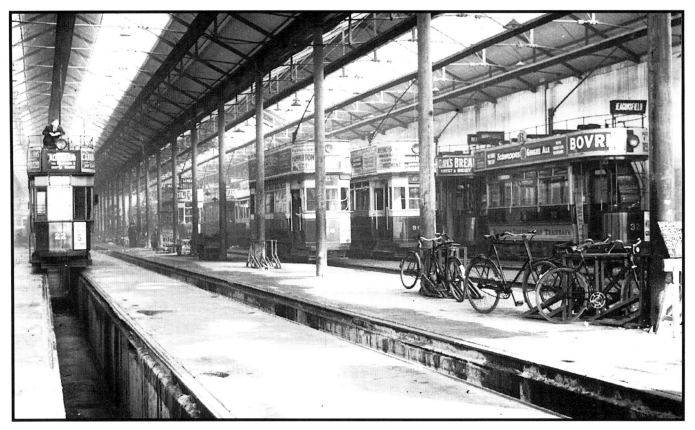

Inside the depot with three stages of tramcar development. On the right the initial design with reversed stairs and a lower upper-deck decency panel. On the left with a hexagonal dash, windscreens and the lower upper-deck decency panel, while in the centre the trams have windscreens, convex rocker panels and higher upper-deck decency panels.

General Manager and Engineer. By this time the Tramway employed 232 members of staff. The Tramway staff were encouraged always to have a smart appearance and large mirrors were erected at the depot for staff to check their appearance before starting their shift. A year later the Tramway Band was formed, playing at events around the area.

One of the first innovations introduced by William Marsh was to introduce a "Circular Tour" car (route T). There were two tours each weekday, one in the morning and one in the afternoon. Intending passengers boarded the car at Aquarium. The whole route is detailed in the Description of Routes near the end of this chapter. If there had been any doubts as to the popularity of this service, they were dispelled on the first day of service. Only the upper deck seating was to be used, so the number of passengers was to be restricted to 26. The service started on 6th July 1905 and when the tramcar stopped at Aquarium to pick up passengers there were more people waiting than the tramcar could take. Hastily another car was arranged to ensure that all the people were able to have a ride. During the first six days of operating the circular tour trams carried an average of 39 passengers per day (somewhat more than the planned limit of 26). The tour, including the stops, lasted two hours and covered a distance of nine miles. The cost of the journey was one shilling, six times that of a long journey ride. The tour proved very popular, on some days as many as four tramcars were needed to carry all the passengers. At this time the Corporation had

four illuminated tramcars, each with over 200 light bulbs fixed to the outside. During the third week of operation of the tourist trams (around 18th July), Brighton was host to a motor racing event and in celebration, the Tramway ran the illuminated tramcars in service around the circular route, during the evening.

At this time, like many tramways, extra revenue was earned by selling advertising space around the upper deck decency panels. For the year 1906 this amounted to £1,500, a welcome addition to the income. At this time the Tramway started making its own destination blinds, changing the earlier black lettering on a white background to white lettering on a black background, making easier for intending passengers to read. The system was also unusual in having its route identification (in Brighton always letters not numbers) mounted on the upper deck at the centre of each side. This was more convenient than the more usual situation at the ends, as when passengers approached the trams turning at Aquarium they saw the side of the tramcars rather than the ends. Brighton was always ready to introduce innovations to help passengers and in 1907 seats on the upper decks were replaced by a "stay-dry" design where a hinged half seat was fitted. This had a counterweight keeping in one position. If the seat was wet the passenger could turn it over, revealing a dry seat. When they left the seat the weight swung the half back to its original position, so that rain fell on the already wet side.

Unusually for the south coast, Brighton had a heavy fall of snow on Boxing Day 1908. As the Tramway did not have a snow-plough the track had to be cleared manually.

An unusual argument broke out in 1907 within the Corporation between the Tramway Department and the Lighting Committee. The Tramway Manager, Mr Marsh, complained that the Tramway was being charged at a higher rate for electricity than commercial operators outside the Corporation, despite being by far the greatest user of electricity. Mr Marsh quoted the Tramway and Railway World that a fair price for tramways to pay for their electricity was 1¼d per unit, the Tramway was actually being charged 1½d per unit. In addition, the Queen's Park Road route was making a loss of £1,000 per annum that could be reduced to £480 by joining the line to the Aquarium terminus. He also recommended introducing a parcels service to increase revenue. The Tramway was also intending to raise all fares by ½d. The consequences of the higher fares were soon felt. The Tramways Committee reported that the revenue in August had fallen by £1,000 compared to the same period the previous year. To save money the Tramways Committee decided to close the Old Steine section for the winter except for station route cars. In September the subject of fares was again raised and it was decided that all 1½d fares would be abolished and replaced by 2d fares. All other fares remained unchanged.

At the end of 1907 it was suggested that an additional route should be opened that ran from west to east, parallel to the coastline (all the existing routes ran roughly south to north, from the coast to inland destinations). It became clear in the discussion that a large majority of the Councillors considered the idea impractical and it was rejected.

Works car number 1 was initially purchased as a snow-broom, but was soon given the wider role of general works car. Here it has taken engineers to repair a broken tram.

Unusually, Brighton had a heavy fall of snow on Boxing Day 1908. Two tramcars, numbers 43 and 46, were fitted with wooden planks in a 'V' form to act as snow ploughs. They toured the system clearing the track, though soon found that the ploughs pushed half the snow away from the track whilst on the other side the snow was pushed over the other rails of the adjacent double track. The Management decided to invest in a dedicated snow-broom. This is believed to have been built in-house and it was ready for the winter in 1910/11.

Unfortunately, the bodies of the first batch of cars deteriorated far sooner than expected. Indeed, after only seven years use it was found that the tramcars were in a very bad condition. They had been constructed from American timber that had been badly prepared, allowing it to rot very quickly. Twelve of the first batch were rebuilt using ash, but then the Tramway found a source of English oak and this was used for rebuilding the remaining eighteen. As well as replacing the original Peckham trucks with much more substantial Brill 21E trucks, it was found necessary to change the original 30hp motors to 40hp (these were again replaced in 1929 with 50hp). Another issue rose from the 1870 Tramways Act. This made the Tramway responsible for the upkeep of the road surface between the rails and for eighteen inches either side. This requirement arose from the horse tram days when the passage of the horse would wear out the road surface (the eighteen inches either side of the rails were included as it was felt that the horses wandered either side of the track). In electric tramway days the only wear that the tramcars did on the road surface was on the tops of the rails. Yet the law was never changed and the Tramway had to repair the road surface that was worn away by other road users. The solution that Brighton Tramway came to was to lay granite blocks in place of the wooded setts. These did not wear, but did make a considerable noise when a horse and cart with steel rimmed wheels ran over them.

At the February 1909 meeting of the Town Council a motion to increase the frequency of the service on the Dyke Road route was discussed. The Tramway Committee had looked into this and reported that this year there was a twelve-minute service compared to a six-minute service the previous year. However, the number of passengers carried on the less frequent service was 10,000 greater than the more frequent service the previous year. Also during the first four weeks of 1909 the receipts were £51 greater with a twelve-minute service than the previous year with a six-minute service. The revenue per car mile had increased by nearly a penny. The motion lost on a vote.

1909 saw another debate over the issue of the price the Tramway Committee paid the Lighting Committee for electricity. The Lighting Committee offered to reduce the price from 1.5d per unit to 1.4d. The Tramway Committee responded by asking for the price to drop to 1.35d per unit. Each Committee presented reports that diverged considerably. The Council decided that the charge should be 1.35d per unit. This represented a saving to the Tramway Department of £1,200 per annum. In November 1910 the price of electricity was further reduced to 1.2d per unit, giving a further saving to the Tramway.

On race days the road at the race course terminus became a parking area, all the trams being in readiness for the end of the meeting. The lower saloon destination carries "Special" while a paper notice tells intending passengers that there is a standard fare of 6d.

The Tramway depot near the end of the Lewes Road route.

The Tramway was doing well. Brighton was growing and the new housing was on the edge of town where people used the trams to commute to work. Passenger numbers were increasing every year. In 1910 there was a move for the convenience of passengers when wooden shelters were built at the termini and some intermediate points, giving protection in inclement weather. The quality of construction was so high that many of these structures have survived well beyond the tramway days to now be bus stop shelters, still used by Brighton people. As an economy measure electric meters were fitted to the tramcars. These could identify those drivers who were wasteful with electric power. They could then be given training on more economical driving styles. There was also a change on the track with Thermite welding replacing fishplates when track was renewed. This change was found to increase the life of the rail by a factor of more than two. Another concern of William Marsh, the Tramway Manager, was the price they paid for electricity. Many tramways generated their own electricity, others purchased it from private electrical Companies. It seems that the Brighton agreement was rather expensive. Possibly due to Mr Marsh's attempt in 1911 the price of electricity for the Tramway dropped by 11% from 1.35d per unit to 1.20d per unit. At the same time the Tramway increased the special race day services to 3d. Profits were at an all-time high, helped by a hot summer and the Coronation of King George V, though most had to be spent on track renewal.

One problem faced by the Tramway was the Queen's Park Road route that had a low number of passengers. The Manager reported that over the previous three years the route had lost £1,300 per year. In 1910 it was suggested that the existing 1d fare should be split into three ½d sections, as this would increase the revenue. Alderman Carden said that twenty other town tramway systems had been approached regarding this problem and only two Managers were in favour, all the others had rejected the idea. There were comments that if ½d fares were introduced on one route then there would be pressure to introduce it to all the routes, with a loss of revenue. He suggested that passengers would only ride on the ½d stages, thus reducing the income. The Tramway would need to increase the number of passengers by a factor of three just to maintain the existing income. The proposal was rejected.

Brighton Corporation received a shock in 1911 when the Brighton United Omnibus Company applied for and obtained a Railless Traction Act to run a trolleybus route from the eastern boundary of Brighton along the cliffs to the village of Rottingdean, some 2½ miles distant. The Corporation, along with Hove Council, were worried that the bus Company might use this as a starting point to introduce their own trolleybus operations in both towns. Negotiations were immediately opened between the three parties and the result was that Brighton Corporation bought out the bus Company. Later in the year both Brighton and Hove then promoted Bills to give them powers to operate buses and trolleybuses. In a typical act of disagreement Brighton favoured trolleybuses while Hove wanted buses. They decided to let the Parliamentary Committee decide which to choose. In the event the Lords Committee approved both buses and trolleybuses.

1912 turned out to be unseasonably cold, leading to a reduction in takings. Countermeasures were introduced including reducing the cost of the Tour Car ticket by half to counter coach competition that offered much more extensive tours that included areas beyond the Tramway network. A further attempt to counter the competition was a link with a coach Company to offer combined through tickets to the Devil's Dyke.

The Tramway Manager reported that meters had been introduced on the tramcars and, with an increase in the standard of maintenance of track, the cost of electricity had reduced from 2.15d per car mile to 1.86d per car mile. However, the cost of electricity at 1.2d per unit was putting an undue burden on the Tramway. The Tramway had also been suffering from a large number of broken axles. A new specification had been introduced with a larger diameter and softer but tougher steel and these had proved most successful. In the last part of 1912 the Tramway had introduced an experiment on several routes where transfer tickets were offered that allowed passengers travelling to the central Railway Station to use their first ticket of a journey as a token when changing cars for a second part of the journey (a system called transfer tickets). The experimental period was declared a success and the system was introduced as a permanent arrangement.

The Corporation introduced a parcels service in 1913. This enabled local people to send parcels and newspapers around the town by tramcar. Letters

In 1913 the Corporation Tramways introduced a parcels service. Parcels could be left at participating shops or given directly to tram conductors. There were arrangements to enable Tramways staff to deliver parcels to addresses away from tram routes.

were excluded as the GPO had a government monopoly of delivering them, but carrying parcels was open to competition. For many tramways this was a very profitable side-line. The relationship with the GPO must have been slightly odd as there was an arrangement whereby Post Office staff could ride on the trams using specially made tokens. These were shaped like coins and exchanged by uniformed GPO staff for a ride on the trams.

The busiest section of the Tramway was the quarter of a mile section between the Pavilion and the Aquarium, as this was the terminal loop for most of the routes. In 1913 it became necessary to relay the track. The new rails were of a heavier section than the originals and new points and crossings were fit-

Car 34, bound for Lewes on route L, is on the Aquarium loop, closely followed by car 1 on route "C" to Elm Grove. This was the terminus for seven routes, so the rails wore quickly and needed replacement in 1913. The Corporation laid a heavier section rail.

Another view of the Aquarium terminus loop, showing how busy the stop was with many different routes sharing the rails.

ted. The rail joints were fixed using the Thermit process and automatic watering was fitted on the curves to reduce noise and extend rail life.

A very profitable part of the operation was race day, when there was a major influx of passengers. In 1913 it was recorded that at the end of a race meet in August, 22 tramcars lined up after the last race and were loaded and set off within 20 minutes, carrying over 20,000 passengers. Such was the demand on race days that as many trams as possible were commandeered for duty, even so demand outstripped supply. The Tramway Management requested the Tramways Committee to authorise the purchase of more tramcars. The Committee agreed, but only to the purchase of three new cars, that the Tramway Manager considered would make very little difference. The Tramway workshop built the new tramcars, numbers 51 to 53 given the designation Class B. They entered service in 1914.

An ominous sign of what was to come was seen in February 1913 when Thomas Tilling Limited demonstrated a double deck Tilling-Stevens petrol-electric omnibus to the Brighton Corporation. The demonstration vehicle ran for three days in Brighton and Hove giving free rides to the public. The Company stated that they proposed to use 40 such omnibuses to provide services in Brighton and Hove. If the Corporations approved, the Company would agree fares with the Corporations and also make considerable wayleave payments or give them a share of the profits. Brighton Corporation also agreed to pay the Company £12,100 for 16 motorbuses and the railless trolley powers that the Company had obtained two years previously.

The Tramway found it necessary to renew much of the track and a schedule of replacing worn rails was introduced that kept any disruption to the tramway service to a minimum. The Tramway Manager, Mr Marsh, was congratulated by the Corporation for the convenient manner in which the replacement was carried out with little disturbance to road traffic users. It was also found that the tourist car service was becoming less popular, mainly due to the fare now costing one shilling. The Tramway introduced a new tour, where passengers could purchase a ticket for a ride around the Ditchling circular route plus one return journey either to Dyke Road, or to Race Hill or to Queens Park terminus. This was by normal scheduled trams and the ticket cost 6d.

The powers to operate buses and trolleybuses came into effect in 1913 and Brighton Corporation invited The Railless Electric Traction Company (R.E.T.) to demonstrate their double deck trolleybuses. In 1914 a 700 yards long temporary route was constructed along London Road and demonstration runs made for the Corporation. The traction development of the time meant that it was drawn by horses after being unloaded from a train in the station goods yard. During the demonstration, one trolley pole picked up current from the live overhead and a chain was trailed on a rail to complete the circuit. Demonstration runs were made for the Corporation and several trips were made by the 40-seat vehicle including an uphill journey. It was estimated that the vehicle managed a top speed of 17mph, far higher than the tramcars could manage. In Hove the Cedes Electric Traction Company Limited erected a demonstration route in the same year, running from Hove railway station to Church Road and carrying Councillors from both Authorities. The trial lasted

The demonstration in Brighton of a "railless tramcar" in 1914. Neither Brighton nor Hove Corporations were impressed and neither agreed to purchase any of the vehicles.

two weeks after which the tramway tracks were reinstated. Any thoughts of co-operation between Hove and Brighton were dispelled when Hove announced a preference for the over-running system of trolley current collection, while Brighton opted for the under-running system. Neither demonstration led to any orders and the experimental lines were removed by 1915. In the event 27 years were to elapse before Brighton Corporation introduced trolleybuses to the town.

Other road traffic had been gradually increasing and by 1914 it was realised that, where there were overhead poles placed in the centre of the road, they created a traffic hazard. A programme was started to replace them with span wire poles mounted in the pavement. Also in 1914 a passenger was injured when he was jolted off a tramcar and fell onto the road.

Work had continued on rebuilding the rotting tramcars and all of the first 30 tramcars had been repaired by 1915. This was all carried out in-house and the engineers gained considerable experience as some of the cars had to be completely rebuilt, replacing every piece of timber. Initially, the substandard American timber was replaced by ash, but later British oak became available and this became the timber of choice. Indeed, some of those rebuilt using ash were subsequently rebuilt around 1920 using oak. The underpowered Peckham trucks were also replaced with the Brill 21E design with two 40hp motors.

One direct consequence of this repair work was that in 1914, when Mr Marsh requested the Tramways Committee to fund new tramcars, he proposed using the acquired skills of his workforce by building them in-house. The Committee agreed to finance three cars (numbers 51, 52 and 53), although Mr Marsh had asked for ten. The new tramcars were built in the Tramway workshops and were broadly similar to the existing fleet. The main design difference was that the Brighton-built tramcars had hexagonal dashes and upper deck ends; and they were equipped with quarter turn direct stairs (the older cars had reversed stairs), while the existing fleet had round dashes and ends. No doubt learning from the previous experiences Brill 21E trucks were chosen, numbers 51 and 52 had 7ft 6in wheelbases while number 53 had a 6ft wheelbase. 53 had 26 seats inside and 28 outside while 51 and 52 each had 28 seats on both decks. They entered service three days before the outbreak of the First World War.

In 1914, soon after the start of the War, cars numbers 12 and 45 were involved in a heavy collision in the depot. This required building a new end on each car. During the repairs both cars were given new direct staircases at both ends. The Tramway was now operating under wartime conditions. At the same time the population of Brighton had a sudden increase as residents moved from London to the south coast, fearing the consequences of Zeppelin raids on the capital. During wartime, public transport systems in Britain suffered from overwork and lack of maintenance. Brighton was no exception. The situation was not made any easier by the lack of spare parts and the demands for taking workers to munition works located at the end of the Lewes Road route on top of the demands going to and from the Army cavalry barracks. To meet the demands, tramcars numbers 41 to 50 had their motors, controllers and trolleys removed, becoming trailers. An interesting procedure was developed. At the Aquarium terminus the tram and trailer would traverse the turning loop and be ready for a return trip. This was not possible at the stub terminus in Lewes Road. The tramway developed a neat solution to the problem. The first car of the day would detach its trailer at the terminus and run around the trailer, returning without it. The next tramcar arriving at the terminus would uncouple its trailer, and couple-up to the waiting trailer, pushing into the stub and being ready to haul it back to Aquarium. The procedure would be repeated for the rest of the day.

In 1915 Thomas Tilling sought permission to run omnibus and charabanc services in Brighton. Up until then the Company had agreement to run an omnibus service in Hove and ran buses to the centre of Brighton. But they were prevented from picking up passengers once they had passed the border between the two Corporations. A competitor, the Brighton and Hove United Omnibus Company, had been granted a licence to run omnibuses in Brighton. The response of Brighton was to refuse, despite the recommendation of the Watch Committee that a licence be granted to Tilling to run charabancs (though not buses). Tilling took the matter to the courts, arguing that the Corporation had not acted properly in reaching their decision. The Court found that the decision by the Corporation in respect of the

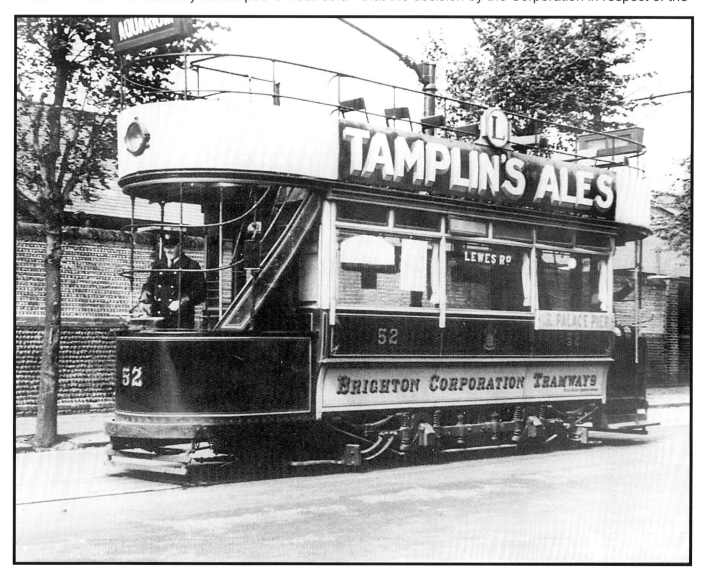

Number 52 was one of the first batch of three cars that were built in-house. The initiative was a success and all subsequent cars were built in the depot.

Tramcar number 52 reaches the race course terminus on a special hire. The driver has changed ends and has just started his return journey using the automatic trolley reverser, much to the entertainment of the upper deck passengers.

omnibuses was reasonable but that the application for the charabanc licence should have been granted. This was a partial success for Tilling, but they still wanted to run omnibuses in the Brighton area. So the Managers of Tilling sought an alternative solution and purchased Brighton and Hove United, thus acquiring the agreement to run omnibuses on the streets of Brighton.

The war also affected the tourist tramcar service that ran from 1914 to 1916 but stopped operating following the Easter holiday in 1917. It stayed closed during 1918, but was resumed in 1919 as a popular entertainment. In 1920 the fare was raised from 1s to 1/6d and this was most unpopular, reducing the numbers of passengers by 50%. As a result, the numbers of passengers on the tourist service continued to decline until October 1925 when the service was ended. However, Mr Marsh was not one to let the inconvenience of the War to influence his forward planning. He felt that the new trolleybuses were the future for the town. So when the tram lines in York Place and London Road were relaid in 1914 the opportunity was taken to remove overhead poles and replace them with rosettes attached to nearby buildings. This was in preparation for conversion of the Tramway to trolleybus operation that would ease the operation of the vehicles in the narrow streets of Brighton. There was still a disagreement between Brighton and Hove Corporations over the type of overhead collection, with Hove favouring the over-running system and Brighton the under-

running. Brighton Corporation decided to refer the matter for arbitration by the Board of Trade.

On the rest of the Tramway, wartime restrictions on spare parts and new tramcars added to the problems for Management. In 1918 the Government required the Tramway to reduce their current consumption by one sixth. This was contrary to the transport demands of workers supporting the war effort. Such were the numbers of passengers that the Tramway actually started building three more tramcars (numbers 54, 55 and 56) using whatever parts were available. For the rest orders were placed with Dick Kerr to be delivered as and when the factory was able to go into tram production, actually not until the end of hostilities. Not helping was an accident involving tramcar number 10, which severely damaged the body of the tramcar. It had to be rebuilt and, unlike the earlier rebuilds, it was not given direct stairs, still retaining its reversed stairs. The accident was unusual and resulted from a misunderstanding. When the tramcar stopped in Queen's Road at the railway station, it was the normal practice for the driver to hold the car on the hill with the handbrake, then change ends. He would apply the handbrake at the other end and when the conductor rang the bell to start the car, the driver rang the gong to tell the conductor to release the handbrake at his end. On this occasion after applying the handbrake on stopping the driver did not change ends, but left the tram to fill his tea can at a nearby café. While he was there a passenger boarding the car accidently put his suitcase on the gong pedal. Unfortunately, the conductor had just rung the bell to start the car. On hearing the gong, he thought the driver was signalling him to release the brake. So the conductor unscrewed the brake and the car started off. After a short while the conductor looked to the front of the car and to his horror saw there was no driver. By this time the tramcar had picked up speed and the brakes were ineffective. The car reached the curve into North Road and was going too fast and derailed. Luckily the car did not overturn and came to a halt about 50 yards further down West Street. Fortunately, no one was injured, but the tramcar was severely damaged.

As soon as hostilities ceased Mr Marsh set about restoring the tramway to its previous condition. He

years the Tramway built 14 new cars, all to the Class B design. The war had also prevented routine maintenance and a seven-year programme of track repairs was set in motion that was estimated to cost £10,000 per annum.

The Manager, Mr Marsh, included an article in Transport World for June 1939 giving a retrospective review of the effect of the War on the Tramway. At the start of 1914 they were expecting a busy Summer season. In anticipation three new tramcars had been built. The War started in July, at the start of the Summer season. Traffic numbers immediately dropped and the situation was made harder in Au-

A wet day in New England Road as car 34 makes its way back from the Dyke Road terminus of route 'N', passing a single track section at Seven Dials.

immediately contacted Dick Kerr with an order for replacement motors for those trams that had been converted to trailers. He was able to tell the Tramway and Railway World that he was first in the queue with his order. However, deliveries were slower than the Tramway wanted and prices had increased by 64% since the start of hostilities. The three new cars were unable to be put into service as their Dick Kerr motors were delayed. In order to resolve the situation Mr Marsh purchased two motors from Westinghouse. The motors intended for 54 and 55 were put into 33 and 36. Over the next three

gust when 40 staff, mainly conductors who were reservists, were sent their mobilisation papers instructing them to report for military service on 4th August. The immediate effect was that on their busiest day of the year, the second day of the August races, nine tramcars had to be left in the depot. To add to the difficulties staff were volunteering for military service, in addition to the reservists. By the end of September 73 staff had left the Tramway. The Tramway was recruiting and training men as quickly as possible, but was unable to cover the vacancies. In line with other tramways in the country, Brighton started recruiting women conductors and 22 entered service in May 1915, the number rising to nearly 100 by the summer of 1918. The number of motormen leaving for the War was less due to Military Service Acts recognising the job as a reserved occupation. An additional worry was that the quality of applicants had deteriorated. Around half the applicants for driver jobs were rejected at the interview stage and over the period of the War some 342 men were accepted for driver training. Of these only 153 were good enough to pass as drivers. The situation regarding conductors was better with 190 men and 360 women being hired during hostilities. The lower staffing numbers meant that employees were expected to work an 11-hour day for seven days a week. The situation was made even more difficult as more factories were changing production to supporting the War effort by making munitions. Spare parts for maintenance became impossible to find, forcing Brighton to cannibalise tramcars for parts for repairs, converting many into trailers. The Government had anticipated that the number of passengers using tramcars would reduce because of the War. In fact, in Brighton over the period of the War the passenger numbers climbed from 10 million to 18½ million per annum (not including wounded soldiers carried free between hospitals and the sea front, estimated at ½ million). The final straw was when the Government restricted coal consumption in 1918.

In 1919 there was an unfortunate accident when a lady passenger fell off the stairway as the car (with direct stairs) accelerated from a stop. She toppled over the dash panel and landed in the road. In order to prevent such an accident, the Tramway modified all the direct stairs tramcars by placing hand rails around the dashes to prevent any passenger from falling in a similar manner. Four of the least reliable cars were scrapped (numbers 1, 7, 17 and 26), while four other tramcars were given decorations of flags of allied countries, no doubt to celebrate the winning of the war. The snowplough (works car number 1) was changed by removing the snow clearing equipment and fitting rail grinders.

It seems that things were starting to get back to normal when the Manager was able to announce in January 1920 that some £7,000 was able to be contributed by the Tramway to the relief of the rates. However, it was reported in April that the Tramway was running a deficit that could reach £30,000 by the end of the year. It was recommended that the 1d fare should be raised to 1½d which should raise sufficient funds to ensure there was no deficit.

Having thanked the women workers on the Tramway for their valuable contribution to the War effort, the mood changed in May 1920 when members of the Tramway Committee decided that all the women conductors should be replaced immediately by unemployed men. Councillor Long said that while women had given excellent service during the War they should now stop doing what was obviously not their work.

On its way back to the Aquarium, car number 12 at the junction of Dyke Road and New England Road.

In the same year the tramway made an application under the Light Railway Act to extend the Lewes Road route on a private right of way to a new housing estate at Moulscombe. In the event the extension was never built, having been rejected in a Corporation vote in 1926. The immediate period after the war saw a steep inflation in living costs, including travelling. Brighton followed suit and applied a general fares increase, including changing the cheapest fare from 1d to 2d. In the first week of applying the new fares the number of passengers car-

Union to the National Joint Industrial Council for the tram-way industry. After hearing both sides the Chairman announced that no decision had been reached.

Unusually, Brighton Corporation came under criti-cism from the Profiteering Committee, who cen-sored the Corporation for charging a shilling fare to take people to the race course on race days. The Mayor pointed out that the route ran at a loss for 300 days a year.

Car 20 at the terminus of routes "C" and "Q" in Upper Rock Gardens. The route was double track with single track sections and a single track stub end terminus. It was one of Brighton's more unusual routes as it involved reversing the car at Race Hill and, while the route was about three miles long the two termini were less than half a mile apart.

ried dropped by 100,000, but the income from fares rose by £154. The issue went back to the main Corporation in April to decide if the Tramway should revert to the old 1d fare. In September the Corporation decided to return to the lower fare for an experimental period of three months. In 1921 ten new cars were built and entered service, allowing eight of the oldest cars to be scrapped. At this time there was a policy of not taking an old car out of service unless there was a new car ready to replace it.

In October 1920 there was dissent in the Tramway workforce when they requested that the Tramway be classified as Grade 1 instead of Grade 2 work (hence eligible for a higher wage). The Tramways Committee rejected the request and must have anticipated problems as they stated that if the men caused further trouble the Tramway would be closed and a fresh set of drivers and conductors would be trained. The issue was taken up by the

In April, May and June 1921 there was a na-tional strike of coal miners, though transport workers did not join it. However, working relations were not good, with high unemployment. This exhibited itself in Brighton when the Tramway staff went on strike for four and a half days in August, followed by a coal shortage in October affecting the supply of electrici-ty to the Tramway. 1922 saw eight new cars being built with three old cars being withdrawn. This year also saw the availability of tramway rails and Mr Marsh decided to renew all the track. In order to en-able the Tramway to continue running a service the pre-war temporary crossovers were used. These enabled cars to cross over to the other track and run "wrong road" while rails were replaced, returning to the correct track when beyond the working area. While the car was on the wrong road the conductor would stand on the upper deck ready to act should the trolley pole (now stretching across the road to its trolley wire) de-wire.

Car number 8 in post-war Brighton sporting its lower saloon curtains. They had been removed during the war. The open dash has the safety rails fitted after a passenger fell over the dash panel when descending the stairs.

The Tramway Manager reported to the Corporation in August 1921 that the Tramway fleet had been restored to the condition it had been before the war. Indeed, in many respects it was in better condition. Since the war 50 new motor tramcars had been built to replace those that were worn out. It was expected that maintenance costs would be reduced as the standard of maintenance had been raised. In September it was announced that, due to falling traffic, the experimental 1d fares would be scrapped and the minimum fare would revert to 2d. The Tramway Committee established an investigation into the feasibility of reducing the number of staff.

In September 1922 the Corporation addressed the criticism of the Profiteering Committee regarding the fare charged to travel to the race course on race days. The Town Clerk told the Corporation that both a 6d or a shilling fare were equally illegal. The Corporation decided that special cars going to the race course on race days would charge 6d but for cars returning before 2.30pm normal fares would be charged. The special service from the railway station to the race course would charge one shilling.

Industrial relations reared their heads again on Sunday 12th August 1923 when the drivers and conductors again went on strike. There were two main grievances, the level of overtime they were required to work was excessive and that the old schedules for the timing of cars should be reintroduced. A meeting took place between representatives of the men and the senior management. It was agreed that the new schedules would be scrapped and the old ones reintroduced and that more men would be employed to reduce the need for overtime. The men went back to work and the Tramway service resumed after a break of only two hours.

Expansion of the Tramway was on the minds of some of the Councillors. A proposal was put forward for the extension of the Lewes Road route to Moulscombe. However, it failed to get the required two-thirds majority of those Councillors present and voting and so the resolution was not carried.

Prior to the war all tramcars were fitted with curtains in the lower saloon. These had been removed during the war. In 1923 they made a reappearance, no doubt giving the passengers the reassurance that things were getting back to normal. More new tramcars were put in service in 1923/4/5, with older cars being withdrawn.

The tram track along Ditchling Road was renewed and granite setts were used to replace the original wooden blocks. This change was to prolong the life of the road surface, as the granite setts were far more hardwearing than the wooden blocks. However, the downside was that they gave a far rougher ride to the other road users and were considerably noisier for residents living along the route. The

Tramway Manager used this work to employ some of the out-of-work men in Brighton and in doing so sought funding for part of the task from the Government Unemployment Grants Committee.

Expansion of the system was in the minds of the Corporation in 1925. The Councillors were expanding the residential area of the town and there was a project in that year to build large numbers of houses in the Moulescoombe area. They proposed building an extension to the Lewes Road route by laying sleeper track on a private right of way to the new housing estate. The sleepered track would allow

When the fleet was increased in 1926 some of the new cars were ordered with vestibules. The tramcars with the windscreens were given the classification Class C. Larger destination boxes were fitted and the headlight moved to the top of the decency panels.

August Bank Holiday in 1925 proved to be a bumper weekend with the Tramway recording a near record sum in takings. However, the Corporation was concerned about the overall financial situation as they applied to the Ministry of Transport for authority to continue with the higher fares beyond the initially

Tram number 40 on the Railway Station route was the first tramcar in the fleet to be fitted with windscreens. It would have been welcomed by passengers and particularly the driver.

great speeds to be obtained, thus reducing journey times to the centre of town. Maintenance costs would be lower than street track and very much less than the cost of running a motor bus service. In February 1925 the Tramways Committee proposed obtaining an Order to enable the track to be laid. A request had also been approved to double the track along Egremont Place and Upper Rock Gardens.

In 1925 the Tramway Committee examined the proposal to fit vestibules (windscreens) to a number of tramcars. While this would increase the comfort for passengers and drivers it would require lengthening existing tramcars and if all the tramcars were so modified they would not all fit into the tram shed. It was decided to convert car number 40 as a trial to see what the benefits would be. Number 40 became the first tramcar to run in Brighton with windscreens.

agreed period. The Ministry agreed, subject to the Corporation giving priority to spending any profits on the proper repair, maintenance and renewal of the Tramway. They were not to make any payment of the revenue to the credit of the Borough Fund or in relief of rates.

In 1926 the income from tram fares was reduced, possibly due to the reduction in passengers caused by the General Strike. The town of Brighton was severely affected by the Southern Railway strike when in May over 80% of workers refused to report for work. Strike action had spread to encompass other public transport workers and on 4th May the people of Brighton found themselves without trains, trams or buses. They could not even read about it as the newspapers had joined the strike. Word got around that the Corporation were considering using volunteers to crew the trams. On 6th May 2,000 people marched on the Town Hall. At around this time the Corporation had prepared at least one tramcar (number 55) for duty. The open platform and lower deck side windows were covered in wire mesh to protect the driver and passengers. While photographs were taken of the tramcar standing on the depot fan, it is unlikely that it actually went into service, or that any other cars were similarly converted. On 11th May a rumour spread that the Corporation was about to start the tram service. Crowds converged on the tram depot to prevent tramcars from leaving. The Corporation was planning to use the day to train the volunteers, not to start running service tramcars. Over 4,000 demonstrators congregated in front of the depot, blocking access. 350 police were sent to the depot, 50 of whom were mounted. The police tried to disperse the crowd and a pitched battle ensued. Men on both sides were injured and 17 were arrested. Five more were arrested in a second brawl. All those arrested were charged and given fines or prison sentences. In fact, the TUC called off the strike on 12th May and instructed members to go back to work. The normal tram service gradually resumed over the next few days.

In the same year, Mr Marsh proposed that the Corporation purchase five 26 seat one-man operated omnibuses to service two routes. The idea was supported by the General Purposes Committee, however, a meeting of the full Corporation rejected the idea by 31 votes to 20. The Corporation was not going to run an omnibus service.

1926 ended unfortunately for a tram driver. He had been summoned for driving the tramway tower wagon, that weighed seven tons, in a manner dangerous to the public. It was alleged that he drove the vehicle around a corner at 15 mph. He admitted he had driven at 12mph, subsequently changing that to seven or eight mph. He was found guilty and fined 20 shillings with 11 shillings costs.

In 1927 a new route was introduced, route C. This travelled across town from Seven Dials to Race Hill where the cars reversed direction. Short working cars would proceed back to Seven Dials, while those working the full route would turn into Queens Park Road to terminate at Upper Rock Gardens.

The system was fitted with trolley reversers at the stub terminals. An innovation that also required alterations to the tramcar trolley poles was introduced by fitting a sliding electrical contact, allowing the pole to be turned without the danger of twisting a wire connection (an improvement that had started in 1918). For safety all the tramcars were converted before the first trolley reverser was fitted in March 1928.

Number 55 with wire mesh protecting the driver and the saloon windows. It is believed that this shows a volunteer being taught how to drive a tramcar. The policeman is clearly there to prevent any trouble. In practice no trams were driven in service by volunteers.

In 1920 a new design of tram joined the fleet. Number 65 was one of four trams classified as Class D that were wider than previous trams and had convex rather than concave rocker panels.

1928 also saw the introduction of a revised design of new tramcar. Recognised as Class D the four new trams, numbers 64 – 67, were four inches wider than previous cars and had convex rocker panels rather than the more conventional concave shape. These changes allowed the cars to have 2 + 1 cross bench seating in the lower saloon, rather than the longitudinal seating of previous cars. They were followed in 1929 by the Class E, numbers 68 – 70, with deeper decency panels, reaching to the upper handrail. The tramcars were longer than the previous cars with 6ft 6in trucks which had smaller wheels than previous cars, of 26in diameter (the previous cars had 30in diameter wheels). The intention was to make access to the lower platforms easier. More powerful 50hp motors were fitted.

At this time more cars were given illuminated decorations, bringing the total to ten. As well as operating on the tourist route, they were also used in normal service, running on all the routes. There was also an initiative to attract more visitors to the resort. The Corporation authorised the funding of illuminations along the sea front and in the valley gardens with electric lights for one or two weeks in the spring and summer. As part of this initiative two more of the

tramcars were selected to be decorated with lights, bringing the total to 12. Each tramcar had 320 lamps of red, green, yellow and blue. They were very popular with the public and illuminated trams ran through to the end of tram operations. In the celebration of "Greater Brighton" week at the end of May the trams joined in the celebrations. They were joined by another tram, decked with flags and bunting that provided a moving platform for the Tramways Band. The 1928 Whitsun proved to be a bumper one, with a record number of passengers for the holidays with 426,503 people being carried, some 120,000 more than the previous year. Takings were up by £680 compared to the previous Whitsun. As a gesture of gratitude to all the Tramways staff each was paid an extra day's pay as a bonus.

Apart from the initial orders the Tramway had constructed all its new tramcars in the depot. The maintenance department were able to construct every part of the trams except the motors, which were purchased from specialist engineering Companies. In 1928 a new design of tramcar was announced when number 68 was built. The trams used by Brighton needed to be powerful as the system had slopes of one in nine and a three-quarters of a mile-long gradient of one in eleven. It proved impractical for the Tilling Omnibus Company to provide a service up such hills and their routes were confined to roads parallel to the seashore. The 1928 tramcar was built with these conditions very much in mind. More powerful motors were used (2 x 50hp compared to the previously used 2 x 40hp). The wheels had a smaller diameter than previously used (26 inch instead of the previous 30 inch diameter). The smaller diameters meant that the tramcar was not faster on level track, but was able to climb hills much faster than the other cars. Number 68 was built with vestibules that were being added to more cars.

In September 1928 there was a warning of what was coming. The General Purposes Committee were asked to consider authorising the relaying of track around Victoria Gardens. They decided to defer any decision for two months and in the meantime to appoint a Sub-Committee to consider the whole future of the Tramway system.

In November the resort was hit by a severe storm, described as the worst since June 1914. The high winds blew down a telegraph pole in Ditchling Road that fell across the tram lines, bringing down the Tramway overhead wires. The pole was carrying overhead telephone trunk wires to London and the force of the impact broke several spans of the Tramway overhead wire. The collapse bent one of the arms of a tramway overhead standard. Luckily there were no trams under the damaged wire, as a tramcar had recently passed. However, the tangle of tramway and telegraph wires took some time to clear and the Tramway service was interrupted for three hours.

The Corporation announced in March 1929 that they were proposing to establish a new Company that would incorporate the municipal tramways with the omnibus services of Thomas Tilling Limited. The new Company would have three Directors from the Corporation and three from Thomas Tilling Ltd. The Chairman would be selected from the Thomas Tilling Directors. The Corporation would invest £30,000 and Thomas Tilling £450,000. The local newspaper reported that there was strong opposition to the proposal from members of the town Corporation who wanted the Tramway to continue giving service. Those wanting to close the Tramway argued that the narrow gauge (3ft 6in) meant that the tramcars could not be remodelled in accordance with modern ideas. Those opposed to the scheme held a meeting of ratepayers on 21st March. A resolution was passed to completely reject the scheme. It was suggested that the Corporation should buy omnibuses to run their own bus service. However, the Corporation continued to support the scheme and made preparations for the merger.

A rare photograph of a tramcar on the 'M' route for the open air market.

In the meantime, the Tramway found that in the August Race Week the high load on the distribution cables had been so great that they were too hot to touch. A similar incident occurred in 1927 and larger capacity cables had been fitted. These now seemed to be inadequate and the Tramway Manager recommended that the engineer be authorised to fit the necessary new cables. The Tramways Committee agreed.

For 26 years the Tramway had a system at Pavilion and Aquarium loops that tramcars travelled in an anti-clockwise direction. This arrangement meant that on the Aquarium loop outgoing trams had to cross over the track of incoming cars. Although it seems to have worked satisfactorily for all that time, in 1929 Mr Marsh decided to introduce a new system where trams would travel in a clockwise direction around both loops. No reason seems to have been given, but it may have reflected the increase in road traffic. The normal Highway Code practice was for vehicles to travel around roundabouts in a clockwise direction, something the other road users would be used to. This change was not just a matter of telling the tram drivers to alter their direction. Substantial changes were needed on both the track and overhead in order to enable this to happen. At the same time the Tramway service needed to continue, particularly as nearly every route was affected by the changes. Mr Marsh planned the changes very carefully. He obtained support from the Portsmouth and Southampton Tramways, with large gangs of skilled track engineers. The whole operation was planned to take place between the end of the day's service on Saturday 4th May and the start of operations on Sunday morning. The scale of the work can be measured by the fact that 22 tons of rails had to be removed and relaid, with new points and crossings. Despite the continual rain throughout the night the workers completed the job in time for the first tramcar of Sunday to run on the new trackwork.

In 1929 another new route was introduced, or rather reintroduced. Early in the life of the tramway a route 'M' (for Market) had been established to serve the open air market between London Road and Ditchling Road. However, at that time, there had been little traffic and the route was closed after a few weeks. The reintroduction proved a success and the route continued in service until a few years before the system closed. The route ran from Seven Dials, along New England Road, Viaduct Road, Union Road, turning into Lewes Road to terminate at Natal Road. It was unusual as it only operated during market hours.

Five new cars, Class E, were built in 1930 and again they incorporated mechanical improvements and more comfort for passengers. A year later saw improvements in the Tramway operation with all main facing points being electrically operated by the driver and overhead frogs being automatically changed by the trolley pole striking a drop arm lever that changed the frog to the required direction. Passengers saw a welcome introduction of reduced fares and five new tramcars. These were Class E, numbers 76 - 80. They had 7ft long wheelbases, the Tramway having recognised that the shorter wheelbase cars tended to "hunt" leading to damage to suspension and track.

the income. So in October the reduced rate return fares were removed and passengers had to pay single fares, making their journeys more expensive. The Tramways Committee calculated that the move would produce an extra income of almost £8,500 per annum. This was accounted for by an increase of nearly 750,000 passengers over the year. Tramway engineers completed the construction of three new cars in the Tramway depot during the year.

Early in 1932 the agreement for the merger of the Brighton Tramways and Thomas Tilling was being finalised. A new Company was formed that had two directors from Brighton Corporation and three

The last five tramcars to join the fleet were 76—80. They were given longer wheelbases to reduce the inclination to "hunt" when being driven.

1930 also saw the formation of a joint transport scheme. It consisted of the Brighton and the Hove Corporations and Thomas Tiling Ltd. Each was to have two representatives sitting on the Board of the new Company.

The Tramway was going from strength to strength and the Manager was able to announce that the Tramway had made substantial profits. He suggested that the fares should be reduced to a universal 1d fare instead of paying income tax on the profits. He considered that with the 1d fare there would still be a considerable sum to relieve the rates. In October a new fare scheme was introduced where the 1½d and 2d fares would be replaced with 2d and 3d return fares. By 1931 the total income from fares had increased, even though most riders had taken advantage of lower price return tickets. However, the Tramways Committee were concerned that the reduced rate return fares had an adverse effect on

Thomas Tilling. Provision was made to allow Hove Corporation to be represented on the Board. Brighton Corporation would have 30/85ths of the profits of the Company while Thomas Tilling would have 55/85ths of the profits (in the final agreement the proportions were 6/17ths to the Corporation and 11/17ths to the Company). There was provision that the Company could abandon the whole or any part of the Tramway subject to agreement of the Corporation to the proposed timetable. The name of the new Company was to be the "Brighton and District Passenger Transport Ltd." However, the merger went to a public vote on two occasions and both times the public rejected it.

1932 also saw four new Class E tramcars, replacing old cars. One of these had been equipped with Allen West regenerative controllers. It would seem that any benefits were not sufficient for these controllers to be adopted as standard. A year later six more

Tram number 74 lies on its side after running away down the Ditchling Road, turning into Union Road and overturning.

new cars were built, replacing four old cars. These cars were designated Class F. A further six Class F tramcars were built in 1933 that had a modified livery. The cream around the windows was extended partly on the side panel and below this the rest of the side was painted maroon. Then in 1934 ten more Class F tramcars were built, replacing ten Class B cars that were scrapped. This was repeated in 1935 with six new cars and another six in 1936. Business was brisk with 24 million passengers carried during the year. By 1936 there were twelve illuminated tramcars.

There was another fatality involving the Tramway in 1935. Tramcar number 74, on route L, was the first tramcar of the day to leave the depot. The rails were wet and slippery and going down the Ditchling Road the driver lost control. He applied the handbrake, but the wheels locked and the car slid down the track and went across red traffic lights at the junction with Upper Lewes Road. Unfortunately, a cyclist waiting at the lights saw them turn green for him and set off, not noticing the tramcar. The tramcar hit him and he was fatally injured. The tram driver had put the motors in reverse and applied power. This caused the points at Union Road to operate and the car turned sharp right, immediately overturning and six passengers were badly injured. The tramcar was so severely damaged it had to be scrapped, even though it was only six years old. The subsequent inquiry held by the Ministry of Transport found no fault

could be attached to the actions of the driver or the condition of the tramcar.

In 1936 the Tramways, Light Railways and Transport Association held its Congress in Brighton on June 10th to 12th at the Hotel Metropole. The Transport World, sponsors of the Congress, published a description of public road transport in the town in their 14th May edition. Omnibus services were operated by the Brighton Hove and District Omnibus Co. Ltd. (set up in 1935 as a subsidiary of Thomas Tilling) working in co-operation with Southdown Motor Services Ltd. The Corporation was wanting to rid itself of its trams and replace them with trolleybuses. By this time the Tramways Department was able to buy its electrical current for just 0.7d per unit. The fleet consisted of 80 tramcars, all built in-house. To improve the riding qualities, a programme had been instigated in 1935 to extend the wheelbase of all the tramcars by one foot. The seating on the tramcars was also being improved by adding Dunlopillo cushions to the wooden seating. The system was run by 250 employees. The profit for 1935 was £4,124 and the maximum fare was 2d, which allowed a transfer to another route to complete the journey. Despite the Corporation having had a Bill to introduce trolleybuses rejected by the House of Lords, they were still intending to make a further application and resolved to convene a meeting of the relevant Sub-Committees to discuss the issue.

By now the questions over the long term life of the Tramway meant just three new cars were built in 1937, replacing three Class B cars. The future of the Tramway began to be questioned in 1930 when a proposal was made to amalgamate the Tramways with the Brighton Omnibus Company and Thomas Tilling buses. Moves were made to obtain Parliamentary approval, but the scheme was thrown out. There was a repeat of the proposal in 1932, but this had the same response. In 1936 a Bill was present-

es was signed on 1st April 1939 and the Corporation lost no time, as the first Tramway abandonment occurred just 26 days later. This was the line along Dyke Road. This came under Hove jurisdiction, so it was replaced with motor buses rather than trolley-buses (Hove objected to overhead wiring). A few days later Mr Marsh, the Tramways General Manager for 34 years, almost all of its life, retired. Mr Winston Robinson, was promoted to General Manager, Brighton Corporation Transport.

A photograph of the beginning of the end of the tram system. The shiny, new trolleybus poses alongside a dated design, open top tramcar. Brighton Corporation acted with undue haste to replace the Tramway.

ed to Parliament to introduce trolleybuses to Brighton and Hove and to abandon the tramways. When it reached the House of Lords it was rejected. In December 1937 the Corporation promoted another Parliamentary Bill to abandon their Tramway and replace the service with trolleybuses. This was given Royal Assent in August 1938 (an agreement had been established between the Brighton Corporation and the Brighton, Hove and District Omnibus Company on jointly operating passenger services on the roads of the area). The revenue earned was to be shared 27.5% to the Corporation and 72.5% to the Company. This was incorporated in the 1938 Act and it was part of the proposals that the Tramway would be abandoned and replaced by trolleybuses. The agreement to convert the Tramway to trolleybus -

Other tramway routes were closed and replaced by 44 Metropolitan-Cammell-Weymann trolleybuses from Motor Bodies Ltd. over the next few months. However, the undue haste resulted in an embarrassing situation, when the trams returned into service to take the race-goers to and from the race track for the August meeting. The last tramcar (number 41) ran on 1st September 1939. The Corporation decided to act precipitously by scrapping the trams as quickly as possible, despite many of them being less than five years old.

The earliest photographs show tramcars without any advertising. However, later ones show that, like many tramways, extra revenue was earned by using the tramcars as mobile advertising boards. Enamel metal advertising signs were fitted to the upper deck decency panels both on the ends and sides of the trams and on the stair risers. In the lower saloon windows paper advertisements promoted businesses and events around the local area. On each end of the lower deck one of the hexagonal dash panels had a paper advertisement and the end windows of the saloons had exterior brackets which held boards advertising local events. Advertising was also placed on the backs of tickets. Most of these were for local businesses, including Volk's Railway. But some, particularly for beer, came from further afield.

DESCRIPTION OF ROUTES

The way in which Brighton Tramway identified its routes was unusual in two respects. Unlike most road public transport, the way routes were classified was by letter rather than the more usual number. The second unusual feature was that the route letter was displayed on the side of the tramcar rather than on the end destination boxes. The reason for this was that most passengers joining the trams at the Aquarium approached from the side and placing the route letter on the destination boxes would have meant that they could not identify which tram was theirs until very close to the vehicles.

The final list of the full route system (only fully developed with the addition of the Market Route C in 1929) was:

B – Aquarium to Five Ways via Beaconsfield Road
C – Upper Rock Gardens to Seven Dials
D – Aquarium to Five Ways via Ditchling Road
E – Aquarium to Race Hill via Elm Grove
L – Aquarium to Natal Road via Lewes Road
M – Seven Dials to Natal Road via Lewes Road
N – Aquarium to Tivoli Crescent via Dyke Road
Q – Aquarium to Upper Rock Gardens via Queen's Park
S – Aquarium to Brighton Station
T – Tour (Aquarium, Race Hill, Ditchling Road, Beaconsfield Road, Tivoli Crescent and back to the Aquarium)

Race Day Specials – Brighton Station to Race Hill

ROUTE B Aquarium to Five Ways via Beaconsfield Road

This route went clockwise around the loop formed by Beaconsfield Road, Preston Drove and Ditchling Road. Starting at Aquarium, the trams went anti-clockwise around Old Steine and anti-clockwise around Victoria Gardens, then up London Road into Beaconsfield Road. Route D ran along the same roads but in the anti-clockwise direction. This must have been confusing for visitors to the town.

Car 27 on Tourist Route duties, where the conductor would also be required to give a commentary, pointing out buildings of interest.

Later in the life of the Tramway the route letters were abandoned. The side destination box shows it is returning to Aquarium from Dyke Road. For the information of visitors to the town there is another side destination board stating "to and from Palace Pier".

ROUTE C – Upper Rock Gardens to Seven Dials

This was the only regular route that did not have the Aquarium as one of its termini and it was not introduced until 1927. Starting at the short stub terminus in Old Shoreham Road the route went along New England Road into Viaduct Road, Union Road, Elm Grove to Race Hill. Here the tramcar needed to reverse in order to be able to enter Queens Park Road and terminate in Upper Rock Gardens. The junction between Elm Grove and Queens Park Road was at an acute angle only allowing tramcars to enter from the east.

ROUTE D Aquarium to Five Ways via Ditchling Road

Route D travelled the same roads as Route B, but in an anti-clockwise direction. This, like route B, had an informal diversion. The tramcars on these route had a tendency to overheat. When a driver found that this was happening he would divert into North Road onto route S, stopping just after the junction. Then he would turn the trolley pole and start driving at the other end of the car, on a cooler controller. As the Aquarium terminus was a turning loop, the cooler controller could be used for the return journey to Preston Drove.

ROUTE E – Aquarium to Race Hill via Elm Grove

Route E started at Aquarium followed the anti-clockwise route around Old Steine into Richmond Terrace and Hannover Gardens turning into Elm Grove and terminating at Race Hill, the highest point on the tramway at 400ft.

ROUTE L – Aquarium to Natal Road via Lewes Road

Leaving Aquarium the route followed the same roads as Routes C and E until they left the Lewes Road to enter Elm Grove. Meanwhile Route L carried along Lewes Road to pass the depot and terminate at Natal Road. The section of track along Lewes Road was the busiest on the Tramway as every tramcar entering or leaving the depot had to travel along it.

ROUTE N – Aquarium to Tivoli Crescent via Dyke Road

The longest route on the Tramway left the Aquarium to travel along London Road bearing left into New England Road then a sharp right into Dyke Road, just before the terminus of Route C, then along Dyke Road to the terminus by Tivoli Crescent.

ROUTE Q – Aquarium to Upper Rock Gardens via Queen's Park

Starting at Aquarium this route followed the same tracks as route E, until reaching the junction with Queen's Park Road. Here the tramcar reversed in order to turn into Queen's Park Road to share the terminus at Upper Rock Gardens with route C.

ROUTE S – Aquarium to Brighton Station

This was the shortest of all the Brighton routes, catering mainly for holiday makers arriving by train and wanting to go to the sea front. Leaving Central Station along Queen's Road, the route turned right into North Road then left to Aquarium where it terminated.

SPECIALS

ROUTE M - MARKET ROUTE

The route serving the open air market between London Road and Ditchling Road. Starting at Seven Dials, it ran along New England Road, Viaduct Road, Union Road, turning into Lewes Road to terminate at Natal Road. It was unusual as it only operated during market hours.

erse the B and D routes. At the end of Ditchling Road a right hand turn took the tramcar into Union Road and then Elm Grove to Race Hill, next to the race course. There was then another 15-minute pause for passengers to admire the extensive views. before returning to Aquarium. The conductor was given an extra duty as he had to become the tour guide, pointing out the main features of interest to the passengers. On busy days, with multiple cars providing the service, some would take the route described, others would traverse the route in reverse order.

RACE DAY SPECIALS

To cater for visitors to the horse racing course on race days, a special service would be run from the railway station to the course at Race Hill. A photograph exists showing a queue of at least 12

Car 41 on a special trip full of local school children. Such outings were often arranged by Sunday Schools. All the children appear to be in their Sunday best clothes.

ROUTE T - TOURIST ROUTE

Run for holiday visitors to the town, this route travelled over the main parts of the Tramway. In order to get the best views, passengers were restricted to the upper deck. Starting at Aquarium they carried holiday makers to the Dyke Road terminus. Here there was a fifteen minute break before the tramcar reversed and went back to New England Road, then reversing again to join Beaconsfield Road and trav-

tramcars waiting at Race Hill having brought crowds to enjoy a day at the races.

NOTE
Except for the terminus at Old Shoreham Road, all the stub end termini were single track, although most of the tramway comprised double track.

BRIGHTON COPORATION TRAMWAYS FLEET

The information given below is based on the very comprehensive tables by Mr R. Knight in "Brighton Corporation Transport Fleet History".

Fleet Number	Manufacturer	Class	Type	Truck	Year Built	Seats
1 - 25	Milnes	A	4 wheel, open top	Peckham	1901	26/26
26 - 30	Milnes	A	Ditto	Peckham	1902	26/26
31 - 40	United Electric Co	A	Ditto	Brush A	1903	26/26
41 - 50*	Dick Kerr	A	Ditto	Brill 21E	1904	26/26
51 - 53	BCT	B	Ditto	Brill 21E	1914	28/28
10**	BCT	B	Ditto	Brill 21E	1917	26/28
54 - 55	BCT	B	Ditto	Brill 21E	1917	26/28
1/7/17/26	BCT	B	Ditto	Brill 21E	1919	26/28
9/11/14	BCT	B	Ditto	Brill 21E	1920	26/28
56 - 58	BCT	B	Ditto	Brill 21E	1920/21	26/28
15/20/23/24/27/30/41/42	BCT	B	Ditto	Brill 21E	1921	26/28
46/49/50	BCT	B	Ditto	Brill 21E	1922	26/28
59-63	BCT	B	Ditto	Brill 21E	1922	26/28
2/36/43/44.47/48	BCT	B	Ditto	Brill 21E	1923	26/28
4/8/16/18/19/21/25/28	BCT	B	Ditto	Brill 21E	1924	26/28
3/5/6/12/33/38/39	BCT	B	Ditto	Brill 21E	1925	26/28
31/32	BCT	B	Ditto	Brill 21E	1926	26/28
34/37/40	BCT	C	Ditto	Brill 21E	1926	26/28
13/22/35/45	BCT	C	Ditto	Brill 21E	1927	26/28
10	BCT	C	Ditto	Brill 21E	1928	26/28
64 - 67	BCT	D	Ditto	Brill 21E	1928	26/28
68 - 70	BCT	E	Ditto	Brill 21E	1929	26/28
71 - 75	BCT	E	Ditto	Brill 21E	1930	26/28
76 - 80	BCT	E	Ditto	Brill 21E	1931	26/28
1/7/17/26	BCT	F	Ditto	Brill 21E	1932	26/28
9/11/41/55/57/58	BCT	F	Ditto	Brill 21E	1933	26/28
14/15/20/42/50/54/56/59/60/63	BCT	F	Ditto	Brill 21E	1934	26/28
2/24/27/30/46/48	BCT	F	Ditto	Brill 21E	1935	26/28
21/23/25/43/49/74	BCT	F	Ditto	Brill 21E	1936	26/28
51 - 53	BCT	F	Ditto	Brill 21E	1937	26/28
1	BCT		Snowplough	Brill 21E	1910	--

NOTES

 * Some of these trams were used as trailers in 1917/18.
** Replacement for withdrawn car

WITHDRAWALS

NOTE   The year in the bracket is when the tramcar(s) entered service:

1917   10 (1901)
1919   1/7/17 (1901); 26 (1902)
1920   9/11/14 (1901)
1921   15/20/23/24 (1901); 27/30 (1902); 41/42 (1904)
1922   46/49/50 (1904)
1923   2 (1901); 36 (1903); 43/44/47/48 (1904)
1924   4/8/16/18/19/21/25 (1901); 28 (1902)
1925   3/5/6/12 (1901); 29 (1902); 33/38/39 (1903)
1926   31/32/34/37/40 (1903)
1927   13/22 (1901; 35 (1903); 45 (1904)
1928   10 (1917)
1932   1/7/17/26 (1919)
1933   55 (1917);9/11(1920); 57/58 (1921); 41 (1921)
1934   54 (1917); 14 (1920); 15/20/42/56 (1921); 50/59/60/63 (1922)
1935   24 (1921); 27/30 (1921); 46 (1922); 2/48 (1923)
1936   23 (1921); 49 (1922); 43 (1923); 21/25 (1924); 74 (1930)
1937   51/52/53 (1914)
1939   61/62 (1922); 36/44/47 (1923); 4/8/16/18/19/28 (1924); 3/5/6/12/29/33/38/39 (1925); 31/32/34/37/40 (1926); 13/22/35/45
         (1927); 10/64/65/66/67 (1928); 68/69/70 (1929); 71/72/73/74/75 (1930); 76/77/78/79/80 (1931); 1/7/17/26 (1932);
         9/11/41/55/57/58 (1933); 14/15/20/42/50/54/56/59/60/63 (1934); 2/24/27/30/46/48 (1935); 21/23/25/43/49/74 (1936);
         51/52/53 (1937)

NOTES

Numbers 1 – 25 (1901) and 26 – 30 (1902) Class A

The first order for cars was placed with G. F. Milnes & Company. The open top, four wheel cars had 90 degree reversed stairs. The lower saloon had three windows each side and longitudinal, plywood seats while on the upper deck were garden seats in a 2 – 1 configuration. Motors were two Westinghouse 30hp fitted to a Peckham truck. The handbrake column was combined with the track brake wheel. The tramcars were unsatisfactory in several ways. As recorded earlier the wood used on the bodies rotted far too quickly; the trucks were heavy on wheel axles, which were prone to shearing in two; and the motors were underpowered for the steep hills of Brighton. As recorded earlier, the bodies had to be rebuilt, the trucks replaced by the Brill 21E design; and 40hp motors fitted.

Numbers 31 – 40 (1903) Class A

The second order was also placed with G. F. Milnes & Company, but the bodies were ordered from Whitting Brothers and were made of British oak. With their experience of the first batch the Corporation specified Brill 21E trucks, but there was an outcry to "buy British" and the order was changed to Brush type A with two 30hp motors. The new trams proved far better than the first batch and, except for a few, ran with their original equipment most of their lives.

Numbers 41 – 46 (1904) 47 – 50 (1905) Class A

Brighton went to United Electric Company for their third order. Similar to the design of the previous orders, there were some detail differences. For example, the stairs were 180° reversed. With their previous experiences the order specified Brill 21E trucks with two 30hp Dick Kerr motors and controllers. As recorded, in 1914-18 earlier ten of these cars had their motors and control gear removed and were used as trailers on the Lewes Road route.

56 tramcars various numbers (1914 - 1925) Class B

By now the staff in the Brighton Tramways workshops had acquired significant experience in rebuilding tramcars, some of which had been almost built entirely from scratch. Mr Marsh clearly came to the conclusion that his workers not only had the necessary skills to build tramcars from scratch, but also by keeping the construction in-house he would be able to maintain his own high quality control standards. No doubt the Tramway Committee had some reservations and initially he was only funded to build three tramcars, numbers 51 – 53. Very similar to the design of the previous cars, the BCT built trams differed in having 90° direct stairs. A single line destination box was fitted above the upper deck handrail at the ends. Those tramcars built after 1919 were fitted with stair handrails that wrapped around above the dash panel, a change brought in by the accident that year when a female passenger fell from the stairs, over the dash onto the road. The earlier tramcars that had direct stairs built prior to 1919 were also modified. Numbers 51 and 52 had two additional seats squeezed in to give 28 + 28 seating. They retained these, though 53 and all later cars had 26 + 28 seating. The lower saloon had longitudinal seating so the number of passengers is somewhat theoretical. In practice more children could be seated than adults and a full tramcar that brakes suddenly can find it has acquired extra space for one passenger each side. The war began a few days after the first three cars entered service and, although they were clearly very successful, a lack of materials meant that no further tramcars were built until 1919. By this time the fleet had been suffering with lack of maintenance and spare parts. Most of the Class B cars built from 1919 were used to replace worn out cars. Only ten of the 56 newly built cars actually added to the total numbers of cars in the fleet.

8 tramcars various numbers (1926 - 1928) Class C

All of these cars were made to replace worn out cars. The main change that was introduced with these cars was that octagonal dashes were fitted. The first four cars built were given destination boxes like the Class B, the others had a three-line destination display built into the upper deck decency panel. This was popular with the public and became the standard for all new and rebuilt cars. Car 40 was given an experimental dash and windscreen that looked like a conservatory built for the driver.

Numbers 64 – 67 (1928) Class D

These cars introduced design changes to the bodies. Convex rocker panels replaced the earlier concave design and the tramcars were four inches wider, that allowed 2 + 1 transverse seating to be used in the lower saloon. The safety of the vehicles was enhanced by fitting Westinghouse air brakes in addition to the track brakes.

17 tramcars various numbers (1929 - 1931) Class E

12 of these cars were additions to the fleet, while the remaining 5 were replacements for old cars. Although other new cars were introduced later it was the Class E cars that had the highest fleet number, 80. These were very similar in design to the Class D, but the Es were fitted with coloured glass in the bulkheads. Initially the Class were built with 26in diameter wheels, to make boarding the cars easier. However, an unfortunate side effect was found, the top speed of the tramcar was significantly lower than those with 33in wheels. Later some of the batch were given the larger wheels. An improvement was to fit some of the class with roller bearing axle boxes.

31 tramcars various numbers (1932 - 1937) Class F

These cars were very similar to the Class E. For the passenger the main difference was in the livery. The cream around the windows was extended to a wide band below the windows. Below this the rocker panels were painted all maroon, while the upper deck decency panels, with hexagonal ends, were painted cream. The cars entering service in 1937 were destined to be scrapped after just two years' service.

LIVERY

1901 – 1918   burgundy and cream. However, red paint is notoriously subject to deterioration in sunlight and the Brighton colour was no different. By 1918 it was decided to change the colour.

1918 – c1926 chocolate and cream.

c1926 – 1939 brighter plum and cream.

ADVERTISEMENTS

The earliest photographs show tramcars without any advertising. However, later ones show that, like many tramways, extra revenue was earned by using the tramcars as mobile advertising boards. Enamel metal advertising signs were fitted to the upper deck decency panels both on the ends and sides of the trams and on the stair risers. In the lower saloon windows paper advertisements promoted businesses and events around the local area. On each end of the lower deck one of the hexagonal dash panels had a paper advertisement and the end windows of the saloons had exterior brackets which held boards advertising local events. Advertising was also placed on the backs of tickets. Most of these were for local businesses, including Volk's Railway. But some, particularly for beer, came from further afield.

DECORATED AND ILLUMINATED TRAMCARS

From the start the Tramway had illuminated tramcars to help publicise the service. Initially there were four cars which were decorated. Over the years this rose to a total of twelve plus additional 'special' cars decorated for special events.

1901	Opening of Tramway
1911	Coronation of King George V
c1911	Visit by French Navy No 19
1929-39	Illuminated cars for Summer and Christmas
c1930	Illuminated Brighton crest
c1930	Visit by French tourists
1937	Coronation of King George VI

SURVIVORS

After the system closed the tramcars were mainly scrapped, though a few were sold as bodies for use as sheds. Number 43 was retained by Brighton Corporation for preservation, however, it was scrapped in 1943 as part of the war effort. Numbers 23, 53, 54 and 63 were sold locally. Number 23 has since been scrapped. The fate of number 53 is not known. Numbers 54 and 63 were acquired by the Worthing Historic Vehicle Group with the aim of using parts from 54 in the restoration of car 63. However, the project was abandoned and both cars were scrapped. Occasionally remains of bodies survived, but attempts to save and restore a vehicle came to nought until 2009. In that year the body of car number 53 was discovered at a farm by Guy Hall. It was acquired by the Brighton Tram 53 Society and is currently under restoration. The story of its subsequent history and that of works car number 1 is detailed in that chapter of this book.

Car number 1 decorated for the Coronation of King George V in 1911. It was used on the tourist route.

CHAPTER 6

PARRY PEOPLE MOVER DEMONSTRATION 1994

People Mover 7 in service in New Road, with number 6 in reserve. *Photograph Gerry Cork.*

Entrepreneur John Parry (based in the West Midlands) was thinking about passenger transport vehicles and the issues regarding pollution and global warming. He investigated the use of battery powered rail vehicles, though he knew that a problem with batteries is that recharging them takes time and it would be best to recharge the batteries when the vehicle was not on duty, that is during the night. However, there was another problem, to run a vehicle all day requires significant numbers of batteries. The batteries also add much more weight to the vehicle, requiring more power to move it; creating a vicious circle. The next thought was another form of rechargeable power, the flywheel. While a flywheel runs down faster than batteries, it can be re-energised in a very short time. His Company, JPM Parry & Associates, built a prototype tram and laid some track in the grounds of his workshop. A power point was fitted by the terminus that the vehicle would connect to and recharge the flywheel. The small vehicle (Mark 1) was able to carry two people and proved the theory was practical. Two further prototypes were built (Mark 2 and Mark 3) and tested. The principle worked and Mr Parry formed a new Company, Parry People Movers Ltd. to market the new form of public transport. started building larger trams. A demonstration line was built in 1992 in the

grounds of the Model Village, Himley Park, Dudley. It was inspected by the Railway Inspectorate and passed for public use in September 1992.

To promote the use of flywheel tramcars the Company set up short demonstration lines around the country including Leicester, Himley Park, Brighton, Swansea, Barking, central Birmingham and Bristol Harbour. The demonstration line in Brighton was opened in 1996 and it ran along New Road by the Brighton Dome. It was a short walk from the terminus of the Volk's Electric Railway. Rumour says that the power at one terminus came from an extension lead plugged into a socket in the nearest building, that happened to be a pub. By the time this demonstration took place Mr Parry had developed what he called his Carpet Track, a portable track system, not unlike a large version of model railway track. The route was just 200 yards long using 2ft gauge track. Temporary fencing had been erected at one end that acted as a 'depot' for the demonstration tramcar (number 7) and a spare (number 6). In all the photos I have seen, the spare was not required. Members of the public were given free rides along the short track and back to the start. The demonstration lasted about four days before it was removed.

The aim of the exercise was to show the system working in an attempt to persuade the nearby Volks Electric Railway to operate a test vehicle on their line. Negotiations were unsuccessful and no more was seen of Mr Parry's trams in Brighton.

Later Parry People Movers Ltd built two power units that ran on the Stourbridge Junction to Stourbridge Town branch. A regular service started there in June 2009 under the operation of Pre-Metro Operations Ltd (PMOL). The original Company, JPM Parry & Associates Ltd., was declared bankrupt by the High Court in July 2013 following an application by HMRC in regard to a debt of £70,000 in unpaid VAT. For the latest information on this company, log on to http://www.friendlycreatives.co.uk/ppm

Having just been built, People Mover number 7 was demonstrated in Birmingham. *Photograph David Haynes.*

TRAMCARS

Number 6 kept as reserve
Number 7 used for the demonstration

LIVERY

No. 6 very pale green and white
No. 7 blue and white

People Mover number 6 was also on show at Brighton, acting as the reserve should number 7 develop any problems. During the demonstration its services were not required. *Photograph Gerry Cork.*

CHAPTER 7

BRIGHTON TRAMCAR NUMBER 53 1939 - DATE

Tramcar 53 when in service, at the Aquarium terminus.

The history of preservation and restoration of Brighton's tramcars has been somewhat chequered. When the system closed in 1939 Brighton Corporation set aside tramcar number 43 for preservation. However, with the coming of the Second World War, it was donated as scrap to assist the war effort. Some other tramcars had been sold to local people, as detailed in chapter 5. In October 1962 the Worthing Historic Vehicle Group acquired the bodies of numbers 54 and 63. They planned to restore number 63, using 54 as a source of parts. The project came to nothing and both tramcars were subsequently scrapped. There was no further action on restoring a Brighton tramcar until March 2010, when Guy Hall founded the Brighton Tram 53 Society with the purpose of restoring the tramcar. It had been found in a barn at Partridge Green Pig Farm in Sussex and is believed to be the last remaining passenger tramcar from the Brighton system.

Tram number 53 was built in 1937. After the tramcar had been in service for just two years, the Brighton Tramways closed. Tram 53 was sold to the pig farm in Partridge Green, West Sussex. It was purchased by a new owner in the 1970s and housed in a shed which has given it some protection from the elements. In 2009 it was seen by Guy Hall who, with the agreement of the owner, set up the Brighton Tramcar 53 Society in 2010 with the aim to restore the tramcar to its former state.

Members of the Society have been actively restoring the tramcar in a rural location. In addition to 53 the Society also has a single deck ex-Graz tramcar number 225. This tram was withdrawn from service in 1988 and was purchased by the Summerlee Museum of Industrial Life to run on their museum tramway with Brussels tramcar 9062, during the restoration of Lanarkshire tramcar 53. In the early 2000s it was no longer required in Summerlee and when The Brighton Tram 53 Society was formed the tramcar was moved to the Brighton site where it has been used as a mess room, workshop, store and source of parts. An early job was to repaint the car from the purple livery it carried in its latter life at Summerlee, to a more appropriate green.

In 2013 the Society applied for a grant to help fund the restoration project from the Preservation of Industrial and Scientific Material (PRISM) fund, but were not successful. It was more successful with the Tramway Museum Society who were able to supply a suitable Brill 21E truck from their collection of tramcar parts. It is estimated that approximately £50,000 is required to complete the project. In an interview with the Brighton Argus newspaper in 2014, Guy Hall, from the Society, detailed the aims of the Society included getting the tramcar running in Brighton. He said that he hoped to be able to lay half a mile of track in Stanmer Park where the tram could run enabling the public to ride on it.

The Society have also been given a third tramcar. This is the only works car that the Brighton fleet had. Car number 1 was sold when the Tramway closed and it became a shed in a Brighton garden. In May 2019 it was dismantled and moved to join number 53.

For the latest information on the Tram 53 Society visit their web site at www.brightontram53.org.uk

The interior of tram 23, showing what number 53 will look like when restored.

Car 53 was withdrawn from service in 1937, had its truck and motors removed and the body was left in the yard for disposal.

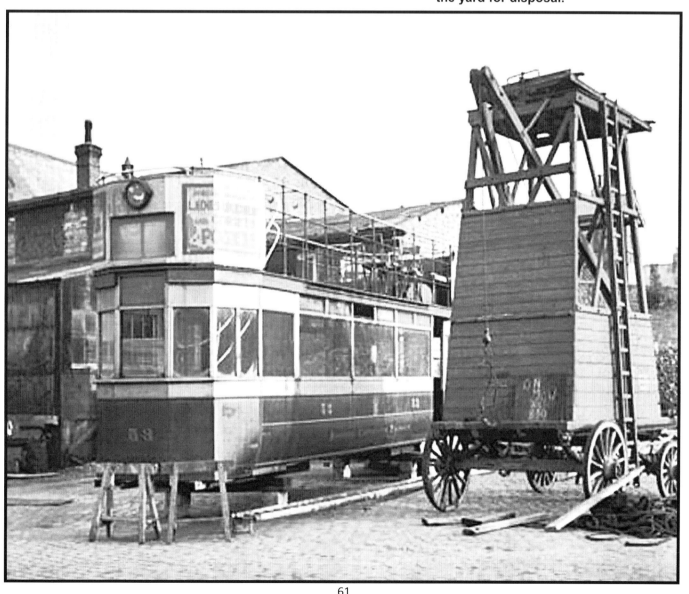

CHAPTER 8

VOLK'S ELECTRIC RAILWAY 1883 - PRESENT

The inaugural run on the opening day of the Volk's Electric Railway at 12 noon on 4th August 1883. Magnus Volk stands on the left hand platform, while honoured guests sit in the carriage waiting for the trip to start.

The father of Magnus Volk (also called Magnus and to avoid confusion referred from now on as "Magnus Elder") was born in 1824 in the village of Langenbach in the German Black Forest to a family of clock makers. By the time Magnus Elder was in his late teens the local industry was under severe threat from competition elsewhere. Like most of the young men of the area the solution was to emigrate. Many went to America, but Magnus had family in Britain so he headed for England. In 1841 he travelled to London and on to Brighton, where there were family friends. He was just eighteen when he arrived but already a skilled clockmaker. He worked for seven years as an assistant to a clockmaker before setting out on his own. Soon after starting his own business he met and courted Sarah Maynard, whom he married in 1850. Magnus Volk was born in October 1851 and he found himself growing up in vastly changing times. In his teens he would have learnt watchmaking skills from his father while the world began to shrink with the, finally, successful, laying of the telegraph cable under the ocean to America. Magnus was then articled to a scientific instrument maker. Magnus Elder died in 1869 at the age of 45. Magnus now found himself the bread winner of the family and had to give up his apprenticeship. He and his mother ran a shop and Magnus started experiment-

ing with the development of a forerunner of the telephone. This consisted of two devices connected by wires. Each had a battery and the users could send messages by activating a needle on the opposite device to move to the left or the right. These represented dots and dashes of the Morse Code. In our eyes it seems very crude, but in the earliest days of electricity it must have seemed like magic. Magnus later developed a "Shocking Coil" that gave electric shocks to unwary victims.

Magnus courted Anna Banfield for several years before they married in 1879, when Magnus was 27. They moved into a house in Preston Road and Magnus was soon bringing in technical innovations. A significant one was to install electric lighting in his house in 1880. There was no generating station and no mains power. Magnus installed a gas motor and electric generator in a shed in the garden to generate his own power. He invented automatic fire alarms, connecting buildings with the local fire station. He also developed an early form of electric motor that he demonstrated at exhibitions. In 1883 he was commissioned to replace the gas lighting in the Brighton Pavilion with electric lights. At the same time, he moved house to Gloucester Place.

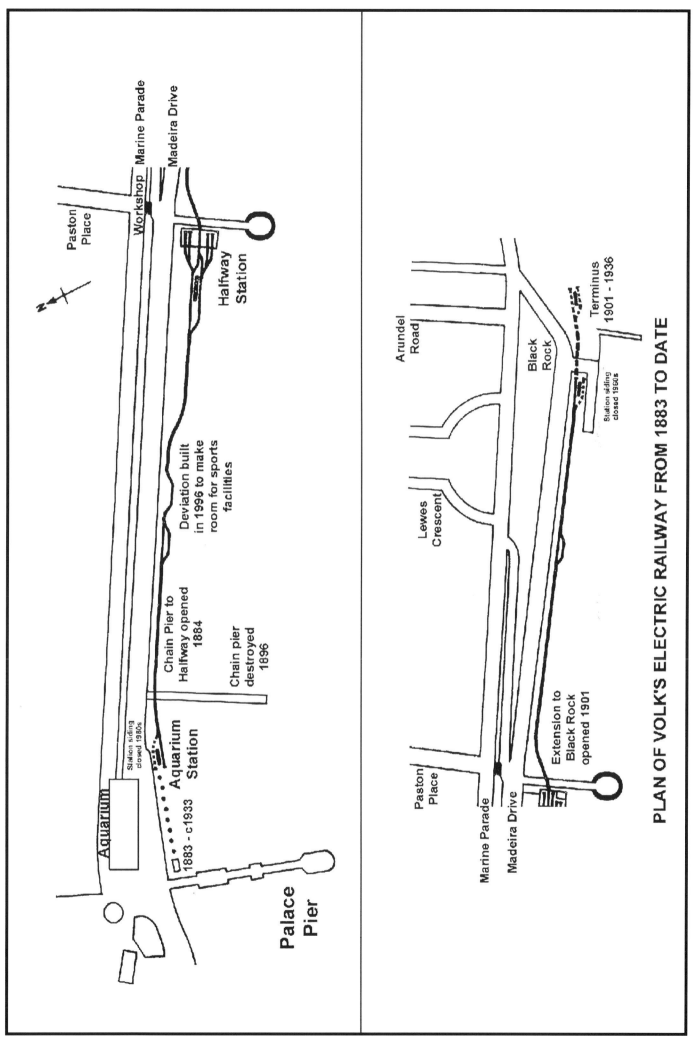

PLAN OF VOLK'S ELECTRIC RAILWAY FROM 1883 TO DATE

In Britain, experiments in using electricity to power transport began with Robert Davidson who, in 1842 demonstrated an electrically powered railed vehicle using batteries to supply the power. It was when the dynamo was invented in 1864 that an accident led to a major advancement. A Belgian engineer connected two dynamos and accidently got his wires crossed. To his surprise when one of the dynamos was spun the other also started turning. He realised that this could be used as a source of power. The first to exploit this phenomenon was Ernst Werner Siemens who, with Johann George Halske, demonstrated a small passenger railway powered by electricity at various exhibitions from 1881. Another similar demonstration was undertaken in 1882 at the Crystal Palace by Henry Bock Binko. This was followed in 1883 by electric power used on a tramway at the National Rifle Association's National Competition held on Wimbledon Common. However, the demonstration was fraught with problems. It was due to commence on 8th July 1883, but it was not able to operate until the following week. A passenger trailer had been converted by fitting an electric motor. However, it did not live up to the promises of its inventor and the demonstration was abandoned. The first successful use of electric power on public tramways or railways in Britain came when the Giant's Causeway electric tramway opened in 1883.

An inspection by the Board of Trade took place on 12th January, though full use of the electrical tramcar did not commence until March. The operation consisted of part electric and part steam locomotive, caused by the use of a third rail electrical supply that could not be used in the town of Portrush.

Meanwhile, Volk's move to Gloucester Place had a significant unexpected effect. It was located within the area covered by the electric mains built by the Hammond Company. This meant that the gas engine and generator Volk had used were redundant. At the same time a customer cancelled an order for an electric motor, that had already been made. Ever ready with ideas he now realised that these three redundant items could be used to make an electric railway. He applied to the Corporation in June 1883 for permission to build a 2ft gauge railway along Madeira Road, or along the beach if preferred. The Corporation agreed to a six-month licence to run a line along the top of the beach from Junction Road, by Palace Pier, to Chain Pier, a distance of under a quarter of a mile. Magnus wasted no time in constructing the line and tramcar. He installed his gas engine and generator in an arch under the promenade used by the Royal Humane Society. The generator was electrically connected to the track, with the 50 volt supply going to one rail and the return

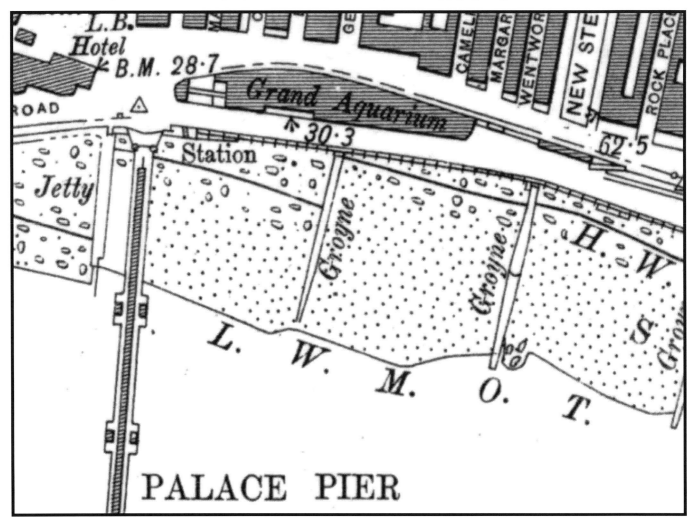

When the original terminus of the Volk's Railway was built in 1883 the Palace Pier had not yet been constructed (it was not opened until 1899). In 1933 the terminus was moved to its present position nearer the eastern end of the Aquarium.

The impact of storms on the seafront line is clearly demonstrated in this September 1903 photograph. The line had suffered similar damage every few years.

from the other rail. The motor was installed in a small four-wheel tramcar that had varnished mahogany sides and blue velvet curtains. It was capable of a top speed of about 6mph. Magnus was able to open to the public at 12 noon on 4th August 1883. A photograph of the opening of the tramway shows eight passengers, though, as five of them were standing in the central gangway, it is possible there were more hidden behind, as the passenger capacity has been given as twelve. The line was an immediate success and extremely well patronised carrying 20,000 passengers over a twelve-week period. It was the second public electrically powered line in Britain and the first on the mainland.

However, new ventures often encounter unexpected difficulties and this was no exception. Four weeks after the opening, on 1st September 1883, there was a storm and the sea washed over the track by the Chain Pier moving the shingle from under the rails, resulting in them being twisted. The tramcar derailed, but swift action by Magnus moved it away to a safer place. The gale damage was just the first of many such events. In the first few years there were damaging storms in December 1884, October 1886, and December 1896. Each time the railway had to be closed while repairs were undertaken.

Despite these interruptions Magnus was most encouraged and applied to the Corporation to extend the line west along the whole of the beach to the Brighton boundary. This was a bit too much for the Corporation and the request was refused.

Undeterred, Magnus immediately applied for permission to extend the line eastward. Outline agreement was given and the line was closed in January 1884 for the improvements to be made. He also rented an arch in the cliff at Paston Place, by Banjo Groyne. This had been excavated in 1837 by the Sussex County Hospital to pump sea water to the hospital for treating patients. He decided to increase the gauge to 2ft 8½in and extend the line under the Chain Pier to reach Paston Place, Kemp Town, a journey of about a mile. In order to pass under Chain Pier, the track had a slope down of 1 in 28 and then up again on a 1 in 14 slope. The track, laid to his new gauge of 2ft 8½in, was single with a passing loop at the centre of the journey, near a request stop. A 12hp Crossley gas engine driving a Siemens generator was fitted in a cave at Paston Place. The power supply continued to use the two rail supply system. He planned to build a funicular lift to link Madeira Drive with the upper road Marine Parade. However, after construction had started there was a surge of antagonistic feeling from the public and Magnus decided to abandon the scheme. He was more successful with the arch he rented in the cliff. It had been given a frontage, a cellar and a first floor. Magnus started using it as his offices, building a balcony on the first floor. As this part of the building was used as his office, the balcony became a useful place to observe the railway and to check that all was operating well. The ground floor was (and still is) used as a workshop for maintaining the tramcars and was initially used as a waiting room for intending passengers.

A new tramcar, number 1, was built in 1884 that carried 30 passengers, 16 within the saloon and seven on each platform. In order to cope with the load a 10hp motor was fitted. Magnus chose to place the tram controller on the ceilings of the car, an unusual feature that persisted until the 1960s. In true Victorian style it was fitted with blue silk curtains, cushions, small mirrors, a clock and a barometer. It was planned to have two tramcars, but only one was initially obtained, to allow it to be tested in service and, if shortcomings were found, they could be improved on the second tramcar. The extension was opened on 4th April 1884 with an official opening on 7th. The second car, number 2, arrived in the summer of 1885, both had enclosed saloons.

The ceiling mounted controller that remained uncovered for over 76 years before being replaced by more conventional tramcar controllers.

It had been found that the two rail electrical supply was prone to causing problems. A combination of salt from the sea air and rain meant that in wet weather there was current leakage across wet sleepers from one rail to the other. To resolve this Magnus decided in 1886 to install a third rail supply, mounting the third rail on insulated supports. As this rail was not load bearing he could use a smaller section (hence less expensive) rail. Typical of Magnus, he chose not to mount his supply rail in the centre of the track or to the outside of the running rails. Instead it was placed between the running rails, but much closer to the seaward side rail than the landward.

Things went well for the railway until January 1887 when the case of Simmons v Volk was heard. Mr

One of the controllers that was replaced by a more conventional tram controller. It clearly demonstrates the live metal that was just a short reach from passengers.

The driving position that drivers had to adopt when the cars had ceiling-mounted controllers.

The first four tramcars lined up for a special photograph. Cars 1 and 2 are at the front and 3 and 4 behind. It was soon found that the winters were too cold and wet for the open sided cars and they were soon rebuilt as semi-open cars.

Simmons sued the railway for damages claiming that when riding a bike along Madeira Road a horse had shied when a tramcar passed and knocked him

Car 2 climbing the ramp having just passed under the Chain Pier.

and if it was bought he would leave Brighton. He did get support from newspapers and his offer was never taken up.

For the next few years he was occupied in working with Moritz Immisch who promoted electric launches from a business at Platt's Eyot, Richmond. In 1889 Magnus moved his family to Richmond. It was here that Magnus met Edward, Prince of Wales, who was interested in trying out one of the electric launches. Magnus kept in touch with the railway and continued to have to fight his corner against a small but vociferous group of Councillors. In February 1892 he moved back to Brighton, where he concluded an agreement with the Corporation regarding the railway.

off his bicycle. The judge found for the plaintiff and awarded compensation against Magnus. This led to many opposed to the railway to renew their efforts to have the railway closed. Two factions, for and against the Tramway, carried out open conflict through the letters pages of the local newspapers. This placed enormous pressure on Magnus to the extent that he offered the railway for sale at £3,700

The Corporation made full use of the power they had in the negotiations, knowing they could unilaterally shut the railway at any time. In November the Corporation agreed to the unique "Brighton and Rottingdean Seashore Electric Tramway". The story of this unusual venture follows in the next chapter. So the Volks Railway story will continue here.

Having returned to the railway, Magnus found that his staff had done a good job of running the enterprise, but had not done any development. One of the first moves by Magnus was to start building two new tramcars. Two chassis, each with a 7hp electric motor and a worm transmission developed by Anthony Reckenzaun, were delivered in June 1892. The bodies were built locally and the two new cars, both to the open sided, crossbench design, numbered 3 and 4, entered service in August. In these days of emphasis on safety, it is difficult to believe that the drive shaft to the worm gear ran through the middle of the seating four inches above the floor. There were two planks of wood either side with the notice "Warning step over shaft"!

The initial line was raised above the shingle beach in order to be level with Madeira Drive. The Corporation built groynes to reverse the erosion of the beach. This has been so successful that the surface of the beach has risen and is now level with the railway track.

The railway fell foul of the weather again during the night of 4th December 1896. There was a great storm that inflicted severe damage to the line. A local newspaper reported that two-thirds of the line were damaged, in some places battered to pieces. Whilst Magnus set about repairing and restoring the track he must have been encouraged by the generous support and sympathy given by the local press. Indeed, the Sussex Daily News began a fund that raised over £100 in the first two days. The line was ready to open in the spring of 1897. At the same time an additional tramcar was under construction and no time was lost in completing it and putting it into service.

In 1901 the status of the railway Company was changed. Until that date it was a private Company owned by Magnus, and hence he was responsible for all debts should it fail, as in the case of the Seashore railway. A private limited Company was formed, shareholders being appointed by invitation (comprising family and friends). This ensured that Magnus would not be made bankrupt if the railway failed. Another encouraging development was the opening of Palace Pier, after many years of construction. This attracted the many tourists who were visiting the pier and Aquarium and who were tempted by a ride on the railway.

In February 1901, after many attempts, Magnus gained agreement from the Corporation to extend the line to Black Rock. At the same time as taking on this expansion, he was seeking solutions to re-open the Rottingdean line. To add to his problems, pressure from a group opposed to the railway persuaded the Corporation to refuse Magus permission to run his trams across Banjo Groyne. This split the railway into two, with passengers having to decamp from one tram walk, across the groyne and board

During storms the journey could become a white knuckle ride with waves pounding the sea wall.

The original terminus Station was considerably closer to Palace Pier. The location was changed in 1933.

town and now Magnus contracted to obtain his electricity from this source. He removed the gas motor and generator and replaced them with a transformer, to convert the supply to 170 volts. When the Corporation Tramways opened in 1901 their system ran on Sundays, something Magnus had been prevented from doing. So he applied to the Corporation for permission to run his line on Sundays. The Corporation had little choice but to agree. So the railway opened on Sundays, with a welcome increase in traffic.

Health and safety in those days was far more lax than today. So the arrangements for the live third rail were somewhat looser. On those sections where the line ran level to the beach, the railway was not fenced off. The public could touch the third rail. As a safety measure the current was only switched on when a tram was moving. There were also designated crossing places. However, where the track was level with the beach the third rails continued across the pedestrian crossings. Where the line was on a bridge the third rail was removed at the pedestrian crossings, the electrical connection going under the track and the tramcar coasted across the gap. Unfortunately, a horse that had been taken to the sea for exercise after an illness, was being taken back when it crossed the railway, accidently standing on the live rail. The shock killed the poor beast, the effect of the shock being made worse by a combination of the wet salt water covering the horse and its recent illness. Magnus demon-

another tram the other side. In fact, Magnus was able to turn a very awkward situation to his advantage. The Corporation wanted to satisfy the opponents but also satisfy Magnus. So he suggested to them that he would not run across the groyne, even though he had laid rails across it, provided the Corporation gave him assurance that they would allow the Tramway to run for seven years. The Corporation were glad to agree in order to see the problem go away. Magnus, quite rightly, was sure that public pressure to allow trams across the groyne would soon make the Corporation change their mind. To run the extension Magnus required three new tramcars and in 1901 he built numbers 6, 7 and 8. In January 1902, as Magnus had expected, a petition of over 300 signatures was given to the Corporation calling for them to agree to the tramcars running in service across Banjo Groyne. The Corporation now had a reason for changing their mind. As soon as this happened, Magnus ran his trams across on the rails he had already laid! To provide sheltered accommodation, the depot was altered by building a roof over the running lines, with doors for security. So the original building could accommodate six cars while the remaining two were stored overnight on the running lines.

1902 also saw a change in the electrical supply. The Corporation had established a DC current supply to the

A car waits at Aquarium Station for its time to start its journey to Black Rock. Above are the flats along Marine Parade, all with a fine view of Volk's Railway.

Car number 9, built in 1910, originally had two doors and a panel on the side facing the sea, while the landward side was left open. In 1923/24 the side panels were removed and it became a crossbench car. Here it is seen at Halfway Station (in its new location slightly away from the depot).

strated to a newspaper reporter that the rail was safe, by placing his thumb and two fingers on the live rail and inviting the reporter to do the same. With some trepidation he did so and found his arm being thrown back by the current. Magnus told him to be firmer and the reporter had a second go, to find the experience a little uncomfortable but no worse. Magnus was fortunate, as the owner of the horse accepted it was an accident and did not take the matter any further.

The line suffered more damage from another storm in September 1903. Almost the whole of the railway line had been badly damaged and extensive repair work was necessary. A brighter event occurred in January 1905 when Herman left the Corporation tramways to join the family firm on the Volk's railway as Engineer and General Manager. He took over the role from Magnus, applying his experience on the Brighton Tramways to the management of Volk's Railway. This continued until 1915 when Herman left the railway to help with the war effort by managing the Gosport Aircraft Company. Magnus returned to manage the railway. He continued to use the Arch at Paston Place, where he could stand on the balcony and view most of the line. He would also make surprise visits, boarding a tramcar to travel along the line. Unknown to him the signal that a tram was about to leave had an unofficial extra code to say that Magnus was on board!

A new car joined the fleet in 1910. This was number 9. To provide it with covered accommodation a novel arrangement had to be introduced. The platform by the ticket office at Halfway was modified to hinge upward and a spur track laid underneath it. This enabled a tramcar to be parked at night under the shelter of the station roof.

The first major accident on the railway occurred on 26th May 1915. Three young lads had been playing in the sea and decided to go home. Rather than walk to a crossing they chose to climb the structure supporting the railway. One boy climbed with no problem, but the second slipped when he reached the track and fell, his neck falling across the live rail. Passers-by who saw what had happened went to aid the lad and took him to hospital, but he was pronounced dead on arrival. As he had just left the sea he was covered in salt water and the effect of the electric shock was stronger than normal. In addition, the inquest found that he suffered from a condition that made him liable to sudden death from a trivial injury. The Coroner recommended that the live rail should be enclosed by wood planks as far as possible and that apart from recognised crossing places the line should be fenced. The jury found that this was a case of accidental death with no blame attributable to any person. They also supported the recommendations of the Coroner. The events had affected Magnus deeply, as the line had run for over 30 years without a fatality.

Events on the railway were uneventful during the war and soon after. At the end of the war Herman returned to work for the railway and help his father. The next major event came in 1920, when the Corporation agreement that the permission to operate the line was about to expire. At the last minute the Corporation agreed to a short extension. But it was not until March 1922 that a longer 21-year agreement was settled upon.

The fleet was expanded in 1926 with the addition of tramcar number 10, an open sided 40 seat cross-bench car. In 1928 the Corporation proposed to widen Madeira Drive and build a swimming pool at the Aquarium, both needing land occupied by the railway. So they gave notice to Magnus to close the Tramway by March 1929. Magnus appealed and was given an extra six months, the notice now moved to the end of September. Magnus and Herman set about seeking support for the railway. They held meetings and gained over 4,600 signatures on a petition calling for the Corporation to reconsider their decision. They did and offered the railway an agreement extending the lease by five years, subject to some relatively minor changes. This included shortening the line to terminate east of the proposed swimming pool. The line was shortened and a new Aquarium station built that opened on 27th June 1930 (ironically the proposed swimming pool was never built. Instead a new pool was opened in 1937 at the other end of the line, also requiring the railway to be shortened.) A new tramcar, number 5 (the existing number 5 having been scrapped in 1928) was built for the occasion. It had an enclosed steel body, which was an unfortunate choice, as it deteriorated under the salty conditions. The official opening was undertaken by the Mayor, who drove the tramcar into the distance, returning five minutes later to the consternation of the official party, as he was only supposed to go a few yards before going back.

At this time the railway had a safety feature. There would be occasions when the railway was very busy

At busy times cars would run in pairs, though sometimes could be separated by a short distance. A simple safety feature was used where the first car of a pair would hang a plate on its front dash. The plate had two triangles pointing up and down. If the driver of a car going in the opposite direction entered a loop and saw the sign he knew that there was a second car coming along the single line section, so would wait until it passed.

and to increase passenger capacity cars would run in pairs, with the extra car slightly behind the scheduled car. As the railway was single track with passing loops, it was necessary to ensure that as cars passed each other on the loop they waited long enough for both cars travelling in the same direction to be in the loop. As a safety measure when a car was being followed it would have a signal plate fixed to its dash. The plate was black with two white triangles painted on it, one pointing up the other down, looking like a diamond with a horizontal line across the middle. This told the driver of the car going in the opposite direction that there was another car behind the first one. In the 1960s the need for this feature was eliminated when the tramcars were modified to run in coupled pairs with just one driver.

Car number 5 was unique in having an all steel body. All the other cars on the railway had wooden bodies. Unfortunately the salt atmosphere corroded the body work and after the closure during the Second World War the tram was found to suffer from advanced corrosion beyond economic repair and had to be scrapped.

much more welcome event came on 4th August 1933, when invited guests met at Aquarium Station to celebrate the Golden Jubilee of the railway. All the guests rode the tramway in special cars to Black Rock and back. Then there were a series of speeches. Selected guests then retired to the Royal Albion for a private lunch.

However, the Corporation was soon back to its old habits and in February 1936 they informed the railway that they would only grant a three-years lease and that was subject to the railway agreeing to rebuild Black Rock Station at their own expense, as the site of the existing station was required for a new, open air swimming pool. The new sta-

The Deputy Mayor has the appearance of driving, but only has his hands on the brake. Magnus is operating the controller that makes the car go.

There was another severe gale in November 1931 causing more damage which took weeks to repair. To attract more custom, the railway organised "son et lumière" and fireworks. In October there was an unwelcome incident when a tramcar derailed while on a raised section of the line. The passengers stranded in the car were unable to walk back along the track, or jump down to the beach. So a second car was sent out with planks of wood. Getting close to the stricken car, the planks were laid over the sleepers and passengers were helped to walk to the rescue car. A

The first station at Black Rock was a simple platform and hut.

The Art Deco station opened in 1937 at Black Rock for the new swimming pool.

tion was opened on 7th May 1937 and a special run was made with the Deputy Mayor on the front platform holding the brake, while Magnus Volk kept a firm hand on the controller. Unfortunately, Magnus passed away a few days later on 20th May.

A new era was dawning when the Brighton Corporation (Transport) Act 1938 was passed, giving the Corporation the powers to operate the railway. Initially the line was leased to Herman Volk, Magnus' son, with a contract where the profits were shared. However, on 1st April 1940 the Corporation took over the operation, promising to keep the name "Volk's Electric Railway". By now the Second

In 1940 an invasion by German forces was a real concern and defences were erected on the beaches of southern England. Brighton was one of the narrowest stretches of the English Channel so the railway was closed, barbed wire laid all along its track-bed and the stations at Halfway and Black Rock were removed.

World War had begun and there were real fears of an invasion by German troops. Beaches around the country were closed, including Brighton beach. Volk's Railway closed on 2nd July 1940 and its buildings demolished and defence barriers erected along the track. It remained this way for the whole of the war. When peace arrived, the railway was in a state of disrepair. The necessary materials were in short supply, but, despite this, the Corporation set about reconstructing the line. Mr E. Budd, former Tramway Permanent Way Manager was brought out of retirement to oversee the operations. It was also necessary to replace the station buildings that had been demolished during the war. At Aquarium a redundant tram shelter was used as a ticket sales office. The tram depot was rebuilt using tramway setts removed when the street Tramway closed. Previously the depot had also been used as a station. Under the rebuilding a new platform was built about 150ft west of the depot. On the platform a shelter was built (just a supported roof which was later removed) with a ticket office. At the time this station was called "Children's Playground" (it has also been called "Peter Pan's Playground"; "Paston Place"; and "Halfway"). At Black Rock a more substantial shelter was built to an Art Deco design, with a ticket sales facility.

By now the fleet was in a sad state of repair and in the winter of 1947 all the cars were moved to Lewes Road trolleybus depot for inspection and repair. The engineers decided that cars 1, 2 and 5 were beyond repair and were scrapped. Number 5 was the newest car in the fleet, being just 17 years old, but the salt atmosphere of the railway had rusted the metal panels beyond repair. This left 3, 4, 6, 7, 8, 9 and 10 which were overhauled. At the same time numbers 8, 9 and 10 were renumbered 5, 2 and 1 respectively. The fleet was re-varnished and given small plastic numbers carried on the edge strip under the ends of the roof. These were difficult to read when new and they became almost impossible when over-painted, making it very difficult to identify individual tramcars in photographs. The tramway now had seven tramcars available for service, which was difficult as a full service with one spare car needed a fleet of nine. At the same time the generator set was changed. A rebuilt 36kw motor generator was installed. The track required renewing and running rails of 50lb per yard rail with 25lb per yard rail for the conducting third rail were used. The railway re-opened to the public on Saturday 15th May 1948 with the service being extended throughout the winter. To reduce costs, during the latter times, drivers also sold tickets.

Coincidently, in 1948 the 3ft gauge Southend Pier Railway was upgraded with new rolling stock. The old stock was sold off in 1949 and Volk's Railway purchased two tramcar trailers, numbers 8 and 9. New to Brighton, they had actually been built in 1898 and were open sided, crossbench vehicles. However, they had two things going for them. They had been completely overhauled in 1911 at the

Brush works and after Southend had sold them to a scrap dealer they were available very cheaply. As they were both trailers the Volk's railway had to undertake some rebuilding to fit motors and control equipment. After refurbishment number 8 entered service in 1950 and number 9 in 1953. They were both given more conventional floor mounted controllers and this may have prompted Brighton to look at the controllers of the original cars in the fleet. Also about 1948 mercury arc rectifiers and transformers were installed, which lasted until 1992.

The two ex-Southend Pier tramcars, numbers 8 and 9 running as a pair. These were the only cars that were purchased second-hand, having worked on the pier for 50 years.

Now that the Corporation was the owner of the railway, it had a change of heart about the eastern terminus. The new station, built when the line was shortened for the new swimming pool, was demolished to enable beach defences to be built. When the railway re-opened after the war a new station was built that was closer to the swimming pool, making it more convenient for the public visiting the pool.

On 11th April 1950 the railway had its second fatal accident, again involving a child. A ten-year-old girl slipped while crossing the track at a proper pedestrian crossing. A tramcar was approaching and the driver blew a warning whistle but was unable to stop in time. The car collided with the girl, killing her. As a result of this, and another fatality a year later, procedures were changed. All the pedestrian crossings were fitted with red lights that flashed when approaching cars activated skids at the side of the track. In some instances, this was supplemented with warning bells. At Banjo Groyne, that had a particularly heavy pedestrian traffic, zig-zag barriers were constructed to prevent anyone from running across the track. A further safety measure was added by erecting fences along the route, with gaps being placed at the crossings.

The pedestrian crossings have traffic lights to protect pedestrians.

Originally the traffic lights at the pedestrian crossings were operated by treadles depressed by the flanges of the tramcar wheel. They have since been replaced by radio signals that switch on the warning lights.

Unusually the controllers were not fitted to the platform floors, but under the canopy roof. The driver would reach up to turn the controller handle. There were seven segments on each controller which connected through resistances of differing values to control the speed of the car. However, the wiper arm, contacts and resistances were all exposed and if the driver touched any of the metal parts he was liable to get an electric shock. A second disadvantage was that unlike normal tramway controllers that had "star wheels" to ensure that the controller handle was always touching the centre of each segment, the Volk's controllers could be left between segments, causing arcing and wearing away the contacts. In the 1950s a programme was instituted to replace the old controllers with more traditional floor mounted ones. The opportunity was also taken to make it much safer by boxing in all of the live parts.

By the end of 1952, the tramcars were needing serious maintenance work. In order to make time to refurbish the tramcars the service ceased in the winter of 1952/53 (indeed the level of takings did not warrant running out of season). The tramway re-opened on 22nd March 1953. Later that year it was decided to reduce the winter service, so on 11th October the tramcars only ran on Saturdays and Sundays. There was a discussion in 1959 for new tramcars to be purchased to strengthen the fleet. However, after careful consideration the decision was taken to keep the existing fleet and to institute a development programme of repair and renovation for the current tramcars.

This allowed the railway to run with two two-car sets on normal days. Adding two more sets allowed a more frequent service on busy days. The operating times of the railway were also changed to 10.00am

New, more conventional controllers were fitted to all the tramcars. However, the usual position for the driver was the controller on the left and the handbrake on the right. On the Volk's railway the positions are reversed.

to 6.30pm, better reflecting its role as a pleasure railway rather than a transport service. Indeed, this was recognised by the Corporation when the responsibility for the railway was moved from the Transport Committee to the Entertainments and Publicity Committee (later renamed Resort Services). An early demonstration of this change came when the fleet was repainted in a new livery in 1962. The old varnish was abandoned and replaced with a yellow and dark brown livery, carrying on the ends and each side of the car large VR letters with the Brighton crest between them.

Car number 6 waits at the Aquarium station. The photograph was taken before the landward side track was lifted.

Seen here in the centenary year 1983 the pair numbers 3 and 4 demonstrate the economical gains achieved by running the cars in paired units.

A later development, available due to the change in the controllers, was running the tramcars coupled in pairs. Apart from the early trailer operation, all tramcars ran as single units. In 1964 the first pair (numbers 1 and 2) were converted so that the controller on the front car operated the motors of both cars. The brakes on the second car were automatically operated by an over-run mechanism. If the second car tried to run faster than the front car, its brakes would automatically be operated. This was a success and, soon after, numbers 3 and 4 were converted, followed by 5 and 7, in 1964, with 8 and 9 being similarly coupled in 1966. As there were an odd number of cars, one car was going to be left unpaired. This was tramcar 6, which was the first car to be renovated under the policy of retaining all the existing tramcars. A subsequent change was to extend the passing loops to enable two paired tram sets to pass and removing the second platform at the termini stations.

In the 1960s - 70s there was a decline in the number of visitors to the resort, that meant fewer passengers using the railway. The appearance of the railway suffered from under investment and neglect. Things got so bad that in 1971 the Chairman of the Kemp Town Conservative Society went to the press to complain that the railway had been neglected so much that it was dilapidated and squalid. He described the tracks as being unsightly and heavily overgrown with weeds. His words had little effect and parts of the track looked abandoned. In the mid-1970s the Corporation were complaining that they had difficulty recruiting staff. Indeed, at times there were only two drivers and a skeleton service had to be run. The Corporation was reluctant to spend on anything except work that was absolutely essential for running. The situation had been exacerbated by the closure of the Black Rock swimming pool and the construction of the Marina starting in 1975. The effect on the railway was profound as it moved from generating a surplus to running at a loss. In the mid-1960s money-saving changes were made, including abandoning and later removing the spur sidings at the Aquarium and Black Rock Stations. An earlier proposal to extend the line westwards to its earlier terminus at Palace Pier was dropped as being too expensive. The line was allowed to decline, with track deteriorating and becoming covered in weeds. It had an abandoned feeling. The Council continued having difficulty recruiting staff. Many ideas were being considered including replacing the railway with a monorail, or a Maglev people mover. These were rejected as too costly and the Corporation decided to keep the line open until 1983, its centenary year. The sting in the tail was that costs would be kept at an absolute minimum. In addition, the bright future anticipated for the marina proved to be false and it was never developed to the extent initially hoped.

The development of the Marina complex was not as successful as had been hoped. Among the initiatives to promote the new facilities Black Rock station was renamed Marina. This photograph was taken in the 1990s when a storm drain scheme meant a temporary relocation of the station about 100 metres west.

A hypermarket was built on part of the area designated for the marina and, probably in a hope to promote it, the eastward railway station was re-named Marina. The re-opening celebration was set for 4th August 1983 and a guest of honour was Conrad Volk, Magnus's youngest son (by now 83 years of age). Two decorated trams, numbers 3 and 4, drove to Marina Station with invited guests.

The railway suffered from arson in 1987 when a fire was started in the depot, damaging tramcars 5, 7 and 2 (the latter severely). By the late 1980s the section of track from the depot to Marina that was built on a viaduct had suffered badly from corrosion. A programme of repair work was set out. The track and top of the viaduct was removed and a concrete raft laid. New track was installed. The work took the winter of 1990/91 and the following spring and summer until it re-opened on 26th August 1991. There were upgradings in 1992 when, as noted earlier, the mercury rectifiers were replaced by more modern solid state rectifiers and the old treadle-operated lights at pedestrian crossings were replaced by new lights operated by radio transmitters.

In the winter of 1980 there was an unexpected event when a cargo ship, the Athena B, was grounded on the shore by the railway. On the 20th January 1980 the ship was heading for Shoreham harbour when it encountered a storm. The entrance to the harbour was narrow and the ship waited just outside the harbour. However, its engines failed and it started to drift towards the shore. The Shoreham lifeboat was called and they rescued half the people on the ship. The remainder were rescued the next morning, leaving the ship to drift onto the beach alongside the railway. It was carrying a load of pumice stone and, as it was now beached, salvagers were able to use a mobile crane to remove the cargo. This operation took several weeks, during which time the ship became a tourist attraction, with thousands visiting the wreck. The wreck had to be given a police guard as some visitors wished to take away some sort of souvenir. Many traders took advantage of the crowds and set up stalls along Madeira Drive. Recognising an opportunity, the Council opened Volk's Railway to give the visitors the opportunity to ride to the wreck.

In the early 1980s a rock concert was held near the Marina that resulted in a fire on the station. The Council decided to close one platform, reducing it to a single track. After a short period, it was realised that this prevented special chartered trains to use the station, blocking the entry for normal service cars. The extra line was reinstated, but declining passenger use and restricted finances meant that the extra platform was closed at the end of the 1980s.

In the 1990s the two ex-Southend Pier tramcars were considered no longer fit for operation and it was decided to remove them. It was determined that car number 8 was no longer needed and it was returned to Southend Pier in 1999 where it was displayed in the open on the pier, advertising the Pier Railway Museum. As it was deteriorating it was decided to move it to Chelmsford Museum after it had been cosmetically restored by Alan Keef with the livery it had when at Southend Pier. Car number 9

One of the ex-Southend Pier tramcars when in service on the Volk's Railway.

was sent to the South Downs Heritage Centre, Hassocks as a static display. However, policy at the museum changed, becoming more of a craft centre, and the tramcar was placed in store. It was then returned to Brighton and to the care of the Volk's Electric Railway Association who have plans for it to be restored to running order.

A major water scheme was begun in 1994 when the Southern Water Services Limited started a £40 million project to build Europe's largest storm tunnel under Brighton. The 20ft diameter tunnel was to be three miles long and 100ft below the surface. The work included building a new pumping station. This affected the railway because the tunnel was to cross the line. The building work was going to particularly affect Marina Station. Indeed, it was necessary to close the existing station and build a temporary station around 100 yards westward. The whole project took four years to build and it was 1998 before the new permanent Marina Station could be opened and the temporary station closed. There was a difficulty as the water Company needed to build their pumping station on the site of the Station. It was agreed that the new pumping station was to incorporate facilities for the Volk's Railway Station. The resulting building is out of scale with the railway. Visitors heading for a ride on the railway see a structure that would not be out of place at a very busy mainline station. On arriving at the Station the visitor discovers that the area dedicated to the railway is miniscule, the rest belongs to the pumping station.

Many local people were deeply concerned about the future of the railway and in 1995 the Volk's Electric Railway Association (VERA) was formed, with the approval of the Corporation, in order to support the Corporation in the ownership and running of the railway. Members of the Society provide direct assistance in the operation and maintenance of the railway and they help to promote the railway to the public. They also have a collection of Volk's Railway memorabilia and other items associated with the railway. The members form a volunteer workforce that gives valuable active support to the railway.

There was a change in the livery of the cars in 2007. As cars were given a repaint the brown and yellow colours were replaced with red and pale ivory. The red was a plum colour that went very well with the pale ivory. The roofs and floors were painted grey. Most cars carry the initials VER on the dashes with the car number beneath the 'E' and some are lined while others are left unlined. Being exposed to the salty air from the sea cars are given frequent repaints to preserve the wood and metal and each repaint results in a slightly different livery.

An initiative to promote the area came with the introduction of "Yellow Wave", a beach sports centre in 2007 on the beach by Kemp Town. The setting up of the sports courts required that the railway track be repositioned. This was carried out by contractors who, unfortunately, used untreated sleepers, which was obviously not a very clever idea given the sea air and damp that a seafront railway has to endure.

Cars 7 and 8 at Black Rock station on a quiet day. They have ben painted in the latest red and pale ivory livery. *Photograph Volk's Electric Railway Association.*

The combination of rain, sea water spray and salt meant that the wooden sleepers deteriorated rapidly. After only 11 or so years the sleepers rotted. The decision was taken to replace all the sleepers from the west end of the Yellow Wave straight to crossing 7 (towards the east). A work team started removing the sleepers in January 2019. A low wall of old sleepers was built to reduce the amount of sand being blown onto the track and getting into the bearings of the trams

The Institution of Mechanical Engineers has a prestigious award scheme for Engineering Heritage. Volk's Electric Railway won the award in October 2012. This coincided with the beginning of the plans for the redevelopment of all the buildings on the line. It was appropriate for display of the plaque to be postponed until the new Visitor Centre at the Aquarium station was opened. In July 2016 there was a presentation ceremony when the plaque was unveiled in the new Visitor Centre. John Wood, Chairman of the Institution's Engineering Heritage Committee presented the plaque to Ian Gledhill, from the Volk's Electric Railway Association Conservation and Support Group, and Stuart Strong from the Volk's Scientific Technical & Educational Group.

The Volk's Railway permanent way has been recognised as a Site of Nature Conservation Importance (SNCI). In 2012 the railway took an initiative to encourage wild flowers by arranging land contouring to encourage small plants by making the dips and crevices that they need to thrive. The aim of the work being done was to enhance the experience for passengers and walkers as they pass through the area either on the train or on the promenade.

In 2013 the Corporation realised that the Railway was facing a very difficult financial situation. The infrastructure and rolling stock were aging and would soon require a substantial investment to carry out essential improvements, not least of which was a new depot as the existing building was unsafe to use. However, like all local authorities the Corporation had limited funding. The Corporation recognised the seriousness of the situation and set aside £250,000 to fund the rebuilding of the depot. In addition, application had been made to the Coastal Communities Fund for £1.47 million. The bid had failed and the Railway reviewed its options. The Corporation then applied for a grant from the Heritage Lottery Fund to pay for:

- Providing a purpose-built heritage visitor centre and ticket office at the Aquarium station, replacing the existing ex-Brighton Corporation tramway shelter that was placed there in the late 1940's.
- Creating a new depot at Halfway with a viewing gallery, new maintenance pits and restoration facilities.
- Restoring three of the cars, Nos. 4, 6 and 10

The plaque commemorating the Institute of Mechanical Engineers Heritage Award won by Volk's Railway and displayed at the Aquarium Station. *Photograph Volk's Electric Railway Association.*

to full working order to increase the service capacity.
- Develop new learning materials and educational sessions for schools.

The initial bid failed, but later a second, revised, bid was made that was successful and in 2014 they were told that they had been awarded £1.6 million. Councillor Geoffrey Bowden, Chair of the city's Economic Development and Culture Committee, said: "Volk's is a truly unique part of Brighton & Hove's heritage and a wonderful attraction, so this funding success is fantastic news. We can now give the railway the tender loving care it deserves and provide an even better experience for visitors and school parties. It's also a tribute to staff and volunteers, past and present, whose dedication has kept the railway on track for 131 years." The railway's manager, Stuart Strong, said: "It is going to be an amazing time ahead for me after 21 years of every day seeing the bigger picture, but not having the funding we needed. I feel so lucky to still be here to see it unfold and to take everyone along on this exciting journey". The grant was enthusiastically welcomed by the Volk's Railway Association.

The Corporation announced a competition for architects to put forward bids for the design and building of the new visitor centre and terminus at the Aquarium. In October 2015 the winner was announced as the Hove based firm ABIR Architects.

On 24th May 2016 tramcar number 4 was taken to Alan Keef's workshop in Ross on Wye for complete restoration as part of the Heritage Lottery funded project. The railway was closed while the car was

Car 4 returned from Alan Keef rebuilt and ready for another 127 years service. *Photograph Volk's Electric Railway Association.*

moved to the pick-up point just east of Banjo Groyne. The whole exercise took 45 minutes after which the lorry began its journey and the railway re-opened. It was followed in early June by numbers 6 and 10. It was expected that the cars would be back by May 2017 (due to unforeseen delays it was not until October that the first completed car, number 4, returned to Brighton).

The railway closed on 4th September 2016 to allow the rebuilding funded by the Heritage Lottery to take place. Television presenter Nick Owen drove the last car set (numbers 7 and 8) before the shutdown, leaving Aquarium at 4pm and going to Marina. The cars then returned to the depot where a small ceremony was held to mark the event. Demolition of the Aquarium Station buildings started on 16th November. The project was delayed early on when an old underground gas pipe at Halfway was discovered during initial demolition work. This had to be disconnected to make the area safe before work could continue.

After being closed for over a year, tramcars were able to run on the portion of the railway between Aquarium and Halfway. On Thursday 12th October 2017 the power was switched on and tramcars numbers 7 and 8 ran over the rails of half the railway. A year's worth of corrosion on the conductor rail made the first journeys interesting, but this was soon overcome as the passage of the tram cleaned the top of the rail.

At Aquarium visitors pass the ticket counter before exiting the station building to the platform to board the car.

Work was still progressing on the depot building and the trams were restricted to stopping at the tram shed, ready to return to Aquarium. Friday 13th was used to show the rebuilt tramway to the media and invited guests. The public service began on Saturday 14th October 2017 using cars 7 and 8. On 11th October 2017 tramcar number 4 had arrived back from Alan Keef with its restored body. It just required a little final fitting out before returning to public service. A Santa Special service was advertised for the weekends in December leading up to Christmas Day.

There was another award for the Volk's Electric Railway Association volunteers on the railway when they were announced as the South East Regional winners of the British Museum Marsh Trust Award for 2017. It was a deserved recognition of the hard work the volunteers contributed to the railway. There was another red letter day on 30th March 2018 when the whole of the railway re-opened. Work on the section between the depot and Marina had been completed on 19th. The trams were able to run through the new depot, where the layout had been changed. The running road now goes through the centre of the depot with storage sheds to the south and a workshop to the north. Slightly to the north of that is a visitors' gallery, enabling people to see work in progress through large windows in the workshop wall.

Certificate awarding Volk's Railway the British Museum Marsh Trust Award. *Photograph Volk's Electric Railway Association.*

Due to the work continuing on the eastern section of the line, the 2017 Santa Express service terminated at Halfway before returning to Aquarium.

direction in the same section. To accommodate this there were two stub sidings at each of the termini. However, with the reduction in passenger numbers, these were removed and the line is now divided into four sections, the first between the single stub at Aquarium Station and the passing loop midway between that Station and Halfway Station. The second section is between that loop and Halfway Station, where there is a second loop. The third section is from Halfway Station to a passing loop midway between that station and Black Rock Station. The fourth and final section is between that loop and the single stun terminus at Black Rock Station. Each track section has its own distinctive token. The procedure that is followed is on leaving Halfway Station, and entering a section ensures that only one tram can occupy a single track section at any time. There are special arrangements should a tram fail and need to be rescued by the works diesel.

Volk's Railway is looking forward to celebrating its 140th anniversary in 2023. The line now has new track, a new Station at Aquarium, a new depot and three completely rebuilt tramcars. Brighton Corporation has a major historic railway that has a very enthusiastic group of volunteers. As the oldest electric railway in the world, it has a major position in the history of railways. Long may it continue to thrive.

When the line is busy cars pass at the loops and the token can be handed directly to the other driver. At less busy times the token would be hung on the pole and the next token taken from the pole at the other end of the loop. *Photograph Volk's Electric Railway Association.*

In 1883 when the tramway re-started operations there was just one tramcar and there was no possibility of meeting another car on the single track. When the track was re-built in 1884 it reopened and soon had two tramcars. As the line was extended more tramcars were built. Once again the line ran using timetables and "line of sight". As safety regulations tightened and alterations to the track meant that parts of the track no longer had a clear view ahead, it became necessary to introduce a token system, similar to that used on single line sections of railways. As mentioned previously, arrangements were used to enable two cars to run in the same

The new depot building showing the access to the public viewing area. *Photograph Volk's Electric Railway Association.*

VOLK'S ELECTRIC RAILWAY FLEET

All Volk's tramcars are single deck four wheel vehicles.

Number	Date Built	Type	Seats	Builder	Motor	Date Scrapped
No Number	1883	Unglazed single deck	10	William Pollard	NK	1884
1	1884	Enclosed	30	Not Known	Siemens 6hp	1946
2	1885	Enclosed	30	Not Known	Siemens 6hp	1946
3 & 4	1892	Crossbench	40	Volk's	7hp 8hp c1901	3 In parts in store 4 Still in service
5(i)	1897	Enclosed	30	Volk's	Siemens 8hp	c1928
5(ii)	1930	Totally enclosed saloon	24	G. Kelsey	8hp	1947
6, 7 & 8(i)	1901	Enclosed saloon	32, later 40	Volk's	8hp	Still in service
8(ii) & 9(ii)	1899 In service 1950 & 1953	Crossbench	40	Falcon Works		See notes
9(i)	1910	Mixed crossbench and enclosed	40	Volk's	8hp	Still in service
10	1926	Crossbench	40	Volk's	Compagnie Electrique Belge 8hp	Still in service
Works	1988 in service 2004	Diesel Works locomotive	N/A	Motor Rail (Alan Keef)	Perkins diesel	Still in service
Works		Welding trailer	N/A	Volk's(?)	None	No longer in service
Works		2 small flat car, 4 wheel trailers	N/A	Volk's(?)	None	Still in service
Works		Longer flat car, 4 wheel trailer	N/A	Volk's(?)	None	Still in service
Works		Tool trailer	N/A	Volk's(?)	None	Still in service

FIRST TRAMCAR 1883 - NO NUMBER

The first tramcar that was run on the Volk's Electric Railway was a small four-wheel tramcar with longitudinal seating for six passengers. In 1883 Magnus Volk contracted Pollards, a local coachbuilder, to construct the 2ft gauge car. Magnus Volk used a 1½ hp electric motor that was left over from a rejected order and he used a Crossley gas engine to power a Siemens generator to provide the 50 volt electric current. He rented one of the arches built into the retaining wall of Madeira Drive to house the generating equipment. As mentioned in the earlier text, the current was supplied using one rail as the positive and the other as the negative, using a small metal brush by each wheel as the pick-ups (the wheels on one side being insulated). The wheelbase was 5ft 6in with very small (14 in) diameter wheels and there appears a lack of any form of suspension. So it must have been a rather rough ride, though the car was only capable of 6mph, although according to the local newspaper the journey was smooth and silent. The tramcar had varnished mahogany sides, blue velvet curtains and a striped canvas roof. The speed of the tramcar was controlled using a variable rheostat that was operated by a removable handle. The tramcar was around 12ft long and 4ft 6in wide. Only the seating area was roofed, the platforms were left with no protection. The Corporation had agreed to the line being built on condition that it was only to run for the summer of 1883 and then it was to be removed. However, the line had proved to be very popular and after Magnus Volk had dismantled the rails he approached the Corporation with a request to rebuild the line for the 1884 season, but to the larger gauge of 2ft 8½in This meant the first tramcar was the wrong gauge and Magnus Volk took the opportunity to build larger tramcars for the wider gauge.

TRAMCARS NUMBERS 1 AND 2 (1885)

When the re-gauged and lengthened 2ft 8½in gauge line opened in 1884 Magnus Volk had purchased a new, larger tramcar, number 1. The saloon was 12ft long with 3ft 6in platforms at each end, 5ft 6in wide and 8ft 6in high. The roof projected over the platforms. Like the first tramcar the body was made of varnished mahogany, lined with gold paint. The tramcar was delivered with four windows in each side of the saloon. This was altered c1905 to two windows to match number 2. The ceiling was painted with flowers by a local artist. The seats were blue cloth with cushions; the windows had roller blinds made of blue and white silk; and the end windows were etched with the Brighton coat of arms and the words "Volk's Electric Railway". The longitudinal seating could hold 16 passengers and a further 7 on each platform. The interior was also equipped with small mirrors, a clock and a barometer. The tram weighed two tons without passengers and still used the two rail method of current supply. There was a controller at each end that was fitted under the canopy that was operated by an insulated handle. The wiring and electrical contacts were uncovered and could give an electric shock if touched. There is no record of the maker of this car or car number 2. However, it is likely that the local coachbuilder Pollard was given the contract for both cars. Along with all the fleet the tramcar was placed in store in 1940. When the tramway was being repaired for re-opening after the war in 1948 the rolling stock was inspected and both numbers 1 and 2 were declared as unserviceable and too far gone to be economically repaired. They were scrapped in Lewes Road trolleybus depot.

A second car, number 2, joined number 1 in 1885. It was a repeat of car number 1 except that the saloon had two windows on each side. It was scrapped with number 1 in 1948.

TRAMCARS NUMBERS 3 AND 4 (1892)

Cars 3 and 4 entered service in August 1892 as open cross-bench vehicles with a worm drive that had been invented by Anthony Reckenzaun. Again these were built locally, probably by the coachbuilder Pollard. The unusual feature of the new drive was that the drive shaft (nearly five inches in diameter) from the motor to the gear box ran through the middle of the seating, protruding four inches above the floor. There were two planks of wood either side of the shaft with the notice "Warning step over shaft". It had been claimed by Reckenzaun that the drive system would last for 20 years. However, despite the gears being immersed in an oil bath, they wore out in just nine years. They were replaced with a more conventional drive system. Probably at the same time the bodies were lengthened to carry 40 passengers and converted to semi-open by fitting sliding doors. Both cars were rebuilt in 2018, number 3 in-house and number 4 by Alan Keef Ltd in Ross-on-Wye. The long-awaited return of Car 4, the railway's oldest car built in 1892, occurred on Thursday 22nd March 2018 when it successfully completed its commissioning trials.

TRAMCAR NUMBER 5 (1897)

The design of this car was a four wheel, four window winter saloon. It was built to meet the increased demand on the railway following the opening of the new line in the spring of 1897. For unknown reasons the car did not seem to be a success and it was withdrawn in 1928.

TRAMCARS NUMBERS 6, 7 AND 8 (1901) 8 was renumbered to 5 in 1948 and back to 8 in 2000

When the line was extended in 1901 to Black Rock more tramcars were needed. Three semi-open cars (number 6 was possibly built as a crossbench car) were purchased to meet the demand. Built to carry 32 seated passengers, they were each equipped with a single 8hp motor that was acquired from "Compagnie Electrique Belge, Liege". During their life the bodies were lengthened to accommodate 40 seated passengers. When the 2017/18 refurbishment was being planned car 6 was identified as one due for rebuilding by Alan Keef Ltd in Ross-on-Wye. It re-entered service in October 2018.

Photograph Volk's Electric Railway Association.

TRAMCARS NUMBERS 8 AND 9 (built 1899 purchased by Volk's 1950)

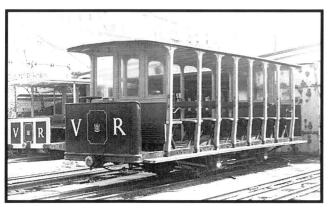

After the war when the tramcars were inspected three cars were found to be in such a poor state they had to be scrapped (numbers 1, 2 and 5). This left the fleet with too few cars. Coincidentally Southend Pier was renewing its pier tramway and sold their old tramcars to a scrap merchant. Volk's Railway were able to purchase two cars. However, they were trailers and work had to be done to motorise them before they could enter service. Numbered 8 and 9 the first car that was ready was car 8 in 1950 and number 9 entered service in 1953. By the 1990s it was found that the cars were beyond economic repair and they were withdrawn. Car 8 was returned to Southend Pier to join the museum. Number 9 went to the South Downs Heritage Centre, Hassocks as a static display. It became surplus to requirements and was returned to VERA and it is currently in store.

TRAMCAR NUMBER 9 (1910) renumbered 2 in 1946 and back to 9 in 2000

Built in 1910 car number 9 was unusual in having the landward side open and the seaward side with panels and two doors. It also had two bulkheads that were retained when the side panels and doors were removed in 1923 making it into a crossbench car. In 1948 it was renumbered to car 2, then in 2000 it was given back its original number 9. In 2002 the car was given a complete refurbishment including new wheels. At the suggestion of VERA it was given 'Pullman' style livery when repainted.

TRAMCAR NUMBER 10 (1926) renumbered 1 in 1948 and back to 10 in 2000

The most recent passenger car is number 10. It was built in-house in 1926 as a standard crossbench tramcar, however, with a slightly more pronounced curve to the roof making it taller than the other cars. In 1984 the body of the car was seen to sway and to strengthen it two bulkheads were added between the roof pillars directly above the wheels. It was identified as one of the three cars included in the lottery refurbishment programme. It was sent to Alan Keefe Ltd in Ross-on-Wye to join numbers 4 and 6 being rebuilt. It was returned to the railway in 2019.

Photograph Volk's Electric Railway Association.

WORKS DIESEL LOCOMOTIVE (no fleet number, but carries works number 40DS530)

The history of this locomotive is intriguing. In 1987 it was the last locomotive ever to be ordered from Motor Rail Ltd., who which was then purchased by Simplex Mechanical Handling Ltd. They sub-contracted the work to Alan Keef Ltd. who built the diesel locomotive for the Butterley Brick Co. Ltd. for operation at their Star Lane Brickworks, Southend-on-Sea. The locomotive was built to the gauge of 2ft. In May 1998 Alan Keef purchased the locomotive when it became surplus to Butterley's requirements. It was regauged to 2ft 8½in and sold to Volk's Railway in June 1998. It is used for all maintenance work on the railway and is particularly useful when the electrical supply to the third rail is switched off.

WELDING TRAILER

This is a four-wheel van that looks like a large, plywood box on railway wheels. Basically it is a mobile cupboard that can be hauled to any part of the Tramway needing work done and especially welding. In inclement weather it doubles up as a shelter for the track team. It appears to have no number; indeed all the support trailers are not numbered.

Photograph Volk's Electric Railway Association.

FLAT WAGONS

There are two small, four wheel, flat wagons. They both have vertical rectangular tubes welded to the sides into which steel bars can be fitted. These support timber planks, converting the wagons into low sided trucks allowing equipment to be carried without danger of any items falling off.

CHAPTER 9

BRIGHTON AND ROTTINGDEAN SEASHORE ELECTRIC TRAMWAY 1889 - 1898

Magnus Volk was clearly very pleased with the success of his Volk's Electric Railway and would have liked to extend it beyond the Banjo Groyne to Rottingdean. However, once beyond Black Rock the beach was bordered by sheer chalk cliffs and the beaches entirely covered by the sea at high tides. Magnus Volk was a man who spurned disadvantages, preferring to change them to advantages. In this case he came up with the radical solution of

that to extend the railway was going to be challenging. He set about examining possibilities. His first idea was to use batteries, but at this time available batteries had a short life and were unreliable. He then thought about conventional tramways and considered using overhead wires. Knowing that water and electricity make a bad mix, he chose to keep the electricity supply clear of the water by placing the positive overhead wire well clear of the water

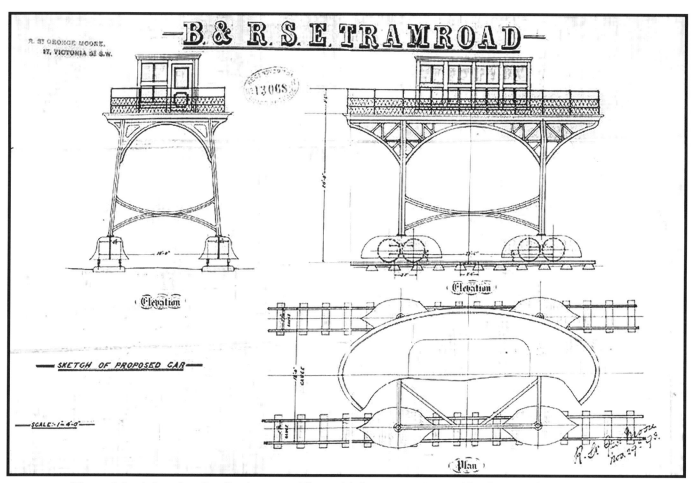

The original drawing for the tramcar. The vehicle as constructed had some detail changes.
Author's collection.

enabling the Tramway to run in the sea at high tides. The solution invented by Magnus Volk was to lay the rails on the beach and allow them to be covered by the sea at high tides. This meant that the tramcar had to be capable of moving through the water, while keeping the passengers dry. The answer was a high platform on stilt like legs that enabled the vehicle to drive through the water, carrying passengers high above the waves. The tramcar is better known as the "Daddy Long-Legs" and it was unique in the world.

The story starts in 1892 as the Volk's Electric Railway was being completed. Magnus Volk realised

while using the rails as the return. The electric motors were to be mounted at the top of two of the legs, driving the wheels by shafts going down the inside of the hollow legs. He designed a tramcar that had all the appearances of a section of a seaside pier. He built a model and met the Board of Trade Inspectors on 18th March to test out their reactions. He recorded that the BoT Inspectors spent considerable time playing with the model. Never had they been asked to approve such an unusual scheme. However, they did authorise its construction, though he did have to agree to a condition that if the Corporation wanted to develop the area he would immediately remove the Tramway. He patent

The tramcar being built in the yard of the Gloucester Railway Carriage and Wagon Company. Note the temporary ladder to enable workmen to reach the high platform.

ed his design in May 1893 and the Act authorising the Tramway was passed on 27th July 1893. The Company was authorised to raise £20,000 capital and £5,000 in loans.

The route of the line was from the Banjo Groyne end of his newly opened Volk's Electric Railway, and extended three miles east to terminate at Rottingdean. Later, an intermediate stop at Ovingdean Gap was added. The design of the passenger carriage meant that a jetty was required at each end of the line. Magnus Volk set about getting the necessary financial backing. The main contributor was Edward Overall Bleacky a resident of Kemp Town and he was appointed Chairman of the Company. They appointed R. St George Moore of Victoria Street, London, as Engineer working with Magnus Volk. Construction of the line began in June 1894, starting at Banjo Groyne. Waiting rooms and offices were constructed on a purpose-built iron jetty and construction of the track began. In common with all aspects of the Tramway, the design of the track was unique. It consisted of two lines of 2ft 8½in gauge set so that the outer rails were 18ft apart. The passenger car required both tracks for stability. Concrete blocks were cast along the line of the Tramway every three feet. They were laid on sound rock and varied in height to accommodate the variations in the base rock. The height of the blocks was such that shift-

ing sand would not interfere with the running of the line. Bolts were embedded in the concrete and 54lbs per yard rails were fixed in place using steel clips. To ensure the gauge was not distorted, tie rods were fitted every ten feet along the straight sections and five feet on curves. Rails were 30ft long with substantial angle fishplates being used to join them. The strength of the track was tested in the winter of 1894-5 when severe gales struck and the track was not damaged. One added complication to the construction was the restriction on the working hours. Access to the track was only available for a few hours a day at low tide. The exact times changed each day and this had to be planned into the building schedule. Access to the works was also a difficulty, with most of the building materials having to be lowered over the cliffs.

One of the first features to be completed was the jetty at Rottingdean. The original concept was for access to the jetty to be from the cliff top. However, before being built, the access was to be from the beach along a long sloping gangway at right angles to the jetty. This gave access to the jetty that ran some 60 feet above the beach to ensure it was well clear of the high tide mark. The main structure of the jetty was built using steel and cast iron, while the access ramp was constructed from wood. At the landward end of the jetty was the ticket office, while at the seaward end was a large platform below which was the steam generator providing power to the whole Tramway. From the platform two flights of steps led down to a loading area that was the correct height for passengers to board the tramcar. The jetty opened to the public on 11th June 1895, nearly

The opening of the Tramway with many illustrious guests watched by a large crowd along the promenade.

eighteen months before the Tramway started running. No doubt Magnus Volk found the income from pier fees very welcome. The generating plant was to become redundant in 1898 when the pier was connected to the Brighton Corporation electricity supply. Later the steam generator with its distinctive chimney was removed, though its building remained to the end of the Tramway.

The overhead electrical supply was another feature unique to the tramway. Initially the vehicle was equipped with a single trolley pole. It seems that the Board of Trade Inspectors recommended that a second trolley pole was fitted,

The short lived terminus building at Banjo Goyne. It was badly damaged in a storm just four days after the Tramway opened.

because if the single trolley pole was damaged when the tide covered the track it would not be possible to rescue the car and passengers. A second trolley pole was fitted, both taking power from the single overhead wire. This is the only example known of a tramcar running with two trolley poles both on a single overhead wire, the return circuit being through the rails, as standard tramway practice. The overhead wire was fixed 36ft above the rails to allow a clear 21ft over the surface of the water at the expected peak tides of 15 feet. The tramcar itself was built by the Gloucester Railway Carriage Company at a cost of £2,000. Each of the four legs had a four-wheel truck, giving a total of sixteen wheels each 33in in diameter. The trucks had metal covers shaped like upside-down boats, the design being such that any obstruction on the track would be pushed to one side. The legs were made from 11in diameter drawn steel tubes 24ft long. They were held rigid by horizontal and diagonal steel struts. The wheelbase was 28ft with a width of 18ft (to match the track gauge). The main structure carried a platform 50ft long by 22ft wide surrounded by a wrought iron fence with a wooden rail. On the centre of the platform was a saloon 25ft by 12ft. There

was a longitudinal bench seat along the centre of the car enabling passengers to view out through the windows. The back of the seats formed a ledge for potted plants (aspidistras and palms). Along the centre of the ceiling ran a clerestory ensuring there was plenty of light inside the saloon. Stairs led to the upper deck that was open to the air, though later a canvas cover could be erected to protect the passengers from the sun and rain. The tramcar had a passenger capacity of 150 people, a record for any tramcar and was given the name "Pioneer", though soon gained the nickname "Daddy Long-Legs".

Pioneer was driven by two 30 horse power, 500 volts electric motors with drive shafts down their respective hollow legs. The power was transmitted to both axles of each truck by gearing. Braking was effected by rods passing through the other two hollow legs. Financially the project was not going quite so well. The building work over-ran the budget and the promotors had to go back to the Board of Trade and get authority to raise more capital and it was agreed that the Company could raise a further £8,000 capital and £2,000 in loans.

The twin tracks laid on concrete blocks that formed a unique tramway line. The rails have long gone, but some of the concrete blocks remain on the beach. *Author's collection.*

The construction of the Tramway was delayed by bad weather, violent storms in the summer and ice forming on the sea in winter, but the line was ready for inspection by September 1896. The Inspectors from the Board of Trade were invited to inspect the line. This added to the unusual aspects of the tramway as the inspection had to be timed according to the tide tables. It took place on 12th September 1896. The first run was carried out at high tide so that the Inspectors could experience the tramway operating in 15ft of water. The Inspectors then waited for low tide and placed obstacles over the track to see how well the tramcar pushed them to one side. The test included piles of timber, concrete, chalk, flint and iron bars. The

The wreckage of the terminal buildings at the Banjo Groyne following the storm just four days after the Tramway opened.

benefit of the town. There was a rumour that, in order to placate some of the local gentry, Magnus Volk arranged for their homes to be supplied with electricity from his power plant.

An opening ceremony took place on 28th November 1896. Local dignitaries attended and they boarded "Pioneer" which started off. But it only travelled a short distance before returning to the groyne as the Mayor was committed to another engagement and left the tram which then carried on with its planned journey. It arrived at the Rottingdean pier some 55 minutes later. The Tramway opened to the public on 30th November with a fare of 6d each way. However, good fortune did not last long. Just four days later, during the night of 4th December, a fierce

tram passed with flying colours. Among the safety features on the tramcar was a telephone that could be used in emergency to call for help. Among a number of minor modifications required by the Inspectors were lifebuoys and a lifeboat. This is the only record of a tramcar carrying such equipment (in fact a total of ten lifebuoys and one lifeboat were fitted, though there is no record of any having to be used). One further unique requirement was demanded. The tramcar needed to be in the charge of a qualified ship's Captain familiar with the coast and able to make judgements regarding travelling in adverse weather. The requirements were implemented by the Tramway and a second inspection took place on 27th November 1896 and the Inspectors agreed to the Tramway opening for public operation, despite some local opposition. One anonymous complainant objected and informed the BoT Inspectors that the passage of the tramcar would be a great source of danger and terror to horses. The Inspectors replied that they had never heard of horses taking fright through the passing of a ship at sea. The Chairman of the Company reported that the first 600 tons of shingle had encountered a storm tide and been washed all over the beach. The Local Authority refused to allow the Company to recover the shingle unless the Tramway could identify their own stones! The Company was obliged to leave their stones on the beach for the

storm hit the area which severely damaged the Tramway, despite "Pioneer" having been lashed to the Rottingdean pier. The storm broke it free and it ran down the line and was blown over. The new installations at the Banjo Groyne were so badly damaged they had to be entirely demolished (as was the Old Chain Pier, the wreckage of which caused the most of the damage to the Tramway). Repairs took seven months and service was started again on 20th July 1897, four weeks after Queen Victoria's Diamond Jubilee. Unfortunately, the Tramway was not insured and suffered a considerable loss over the incident. To save costs, the rebuilt Brighton terminus jetty was far smaller and was sited off the side of the Banjo Groyne. It did not have a waiting room or offices, merely a small booth selling tickets

The replacement jetty at the Banjo Groyne was far less elaborate than the one that was lost in the storm. Just a short platform with no shelter for the public.

A rare close-up view of the overhead wire support. Note the collapsible seats that were raised when the tramcar was full.

prise and Magnus Volk only found out about it after the event. So he rushed to the Tramway and persuaded the Royal Party to undertake a second trip in the afternoon, when he could properly welcome them. He then had a large photograph of the journey and a commemorative plaque placed prominently in the saloon of Pioneer.

Also in 1898 came a challenge from an unexpected direction. An opposition MP, Mr Gibson Bowles questioned the BoT regarding the legitimacy of both the Volk's Electric Railway and the Brighton and Rottingdean Seashore Electric Tramway. He claimed that the former had no authority to operate and that the electric overhead of the latter contravened its Act and the track created an obstacle for people going into the sea. All this was rejected by Parliament and the subject was dropped.

The reconstruction of the line included a new jetty at Ovingdean Gap. This was similar in design to the Rottingdean jetty. However, it was constructed of wood and not steel. The new jetty was ready for the re-opening of the Tramway. Unusually, the jetty was used as a request stop. In practice it was seldom used

The Tramway gained royal approval when the Prince of Wales (later King Edward VII) had two rides on 20th February 1898. The first trip was a sur-

In normal operation the Tramway proved financially unsatisfactory. The tramcar was said to be underpowered and was only able to manage 4-5 mph. This made each return journey last an hour and ten minutes. This severely limited earnings, particularly as there was only one tramcar in the fleet. To increase income, necessary to recoup the losses caused by the storm damage, the journeys were shortened, so passengers just experienced a short passage from Banjo Groyne before returning back. Long enough for them to get the feeling of travelling over the sea, but quick enough to generate more income. There had been talk of adding a second tramcar to the Tramway but it is difficult to see how it could run without laying a parallel track. In the event the Company did not have sufficient money to fund such an expansion.

Crowds wait on the Banjo Groyne jetty as "Pioneer" approaches at high tide.

The jetty at Rottingdean with Pioneer taking on passengers.

Brighton Council had been extending its sea defences by building extra concrete groynes along the stretch of coast used by the Tramway. These altered the tidal erosion and sand and stones were deposited over the tram track. In 1900 the Tramway had to close for five weeks in the peak Summer period in order to effect repairs. Then the following September the Corporation gave notice to the Tramway to move its track seaward to enable groynes to be extended. The Tramway realised that such a move was not practical and they suggested an alternative to move the Brighton terminus to Black Rock and extend the Volk's Railway to keep the connection. The Corporation were impatient and under their powers in the Act began removing track from the area they were working. As there was no pier at Black Rock, the Tramway was obliged to cease operating. It was decided to discontinue the Tramway and application was made to Parliament to abandon it and extend the Volk's Railway by 2¼ miles to Rot-

A ride on Pioneer at high tide would have felt like an ocean going-cruise. The single trolley pole indicates this photograph was taken before the line was open to the public.

tingdean. They were granted the Act on 23rd June 1902. Magnus Volk tried to raise the necessary £40,000 capital. However, by 1906 he accepted that he was not going to be able to raise a sufficient sum in time and he had to abandon the Act.

"Pioneer" was lashed to the pier at Ovingdean Gap and remained there for many years, slowly rotting away. Magnus Volk appears to have abandoned the enterprise and left it to slowly disintegrate. It stayed there until 1905 when J. J. Clark, a former Director of the Tramway, started the removal of the Tramway. The accesses from the shore end of the Ovingdean and Rottingdean jetties were removed to prevent the public entering. Later, the jetties and rails were removed for scrap. One last irony is that the scrap metal was purchased by firms in Germany and could well have been returned in the form of bombs in the First World War. Today the only reminder of the line are a number of concrete blocks roughly in their original places and visible at low tide.

FLEET

Single vehicle "Pioneer".

LIVERY

Black, white and light brown.

The advertising poster for the Seashore Tramway.

Pioneer stands abandoned and lashed to the end of the jetty at Ovingdean Gap. The landward end of the jetty had been cut to prevent access to the tramcar. It stayed here, slowly rotting away, until it and the jetty were demolished and sold for scrap.

CHAPTER 10

GLYNDE TELPHERAGE AERIAL TRAMWAY 1885 – c1899

The purpose of the Glynde Telpherage Aerial Tramway was to transport clay from the clay pits to Glynde Station on the London, Brighton and South Coast Railway.

Professor Henry Charles Fleeming-Jenkin, of Edinburgh University, gave a talk to the Cleveland Engineers on 20th April 1885 on the Telpherage Aerial Tramway. He said that the Tramway had been designed as an electrically powered, overhead line for the bulk transport of goods. He told the audience that the first such line was being built at Glynde, Sussex by The Telpherage Company Limited who contracted. Messrs Wilson, Pease and Co, of the Tees Ironworks to undertake the main works. The one-mile long line was to link the local clay pit with railway sidings at Glynde Railway Station goods yard. The clay was then taken by the railway to the Sussex Portland Cement Company works at South Heighton near Newhaven. The Telpherage system, invented by Professor Fleeming-Jenkin in 1882, differed from other cableways as each train of trucks had its own electric motor unit, rather than the more

conventional continuous moving cable. An ingenious system was used to supply electrical power. The carrying rods carried both the positive and negative supplies as is described later. This was a very early use of electricity in transport. Indeed, the Glynde Tramway was the first electrically powered cableway in the world. Wooden pylons were set 66ft apart carrying ¾ inch diameter steel rods that formed the running rail, that was suspended 18ft above the ground. Unfortunately, Professor Fleeming-Jenkin died during the construction and did not see his invention in operation. His role of Engineer was taken by Professor John Perry.

The manner in which the line worked was very different from the more traditional type of wire-rope haulage systems. Between the pylons were the carrying rails, each of which was electrically insulated from those either side. The rails were electrically connected so that they were alternately positive or negative (see diagram). Each train had ten skeps (as the buckets were called) that were set five each side of the locomotive. All the skeps, except the first, had two insulated carrying wheels. The first skep had one insulated wheel and one that picked up current from the carrying rail. The central locomotive also had one insulated wheel and one uninsulated

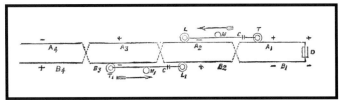

The electric supply system enabling the monorail to operate on a single rail.

wheel connected to the motor. The distance between the first skep and the locomotive was exactly equal to the distance between the pylons. In operation, the tram would straddle two carrying rods, so that the front wheel of the tram and that on the locomotive were on different polarity rods thus providing

The formal opening of the Telpher line was held on 17th October 1885 (the Opening Ceremony for the cement works had been held five weeks earlier on 11th September), with a large number of scientists having been invited. The party began by watching Lady Hampden formally open the Tramway by

Lady Hampden opened the tramway on 17th October 1885 surrounded by distinguished guests.

power to the motor. As the tram travelled along the rails both collecting wheels would move across to new rods at the same time. This would reverse the polarity on the motor, however, this did not affect the motor which continued to rotate in the same direction. The trams could be reversed by altering the positions of the commutator brushes on the motor. The voltage of the line was 200 volts and the motor required some eight amps of power.

In operation a tram would automatically arrive at the clay field where the line sloped down to the ground. A labourer switched off the power to the locomotive, bringing the tram to a halt. The skeps were filled with clay and then the motor was switched on and the tram started off. It automatically ran to the transfer sidings at Glynde Station yard. Here the rods ran over a railway siding. An empty train of open wagons would wait under the Telpher track as the skeps passed over it. Without stopping, a lever on the skeps would strike a post causing the bucket to tip and empty the clay into the railway wagon. The skeps would continue around the return loop to travel back to the clay field.

pressing a button that started the Tramway and the 'skeps' began moving, unloading their clay into rail-

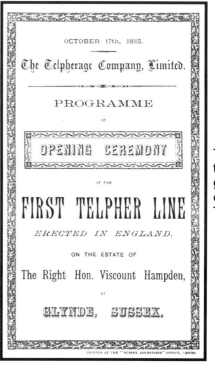

OCTOBER 17th, 1885.

The Telpherage Company, Limited.

PROGRAMME

OF

OPENING CEREMONY

OF THE

FIRST TELPHER LINE

ERECTED IN ENGLAND,

ON THE ESTATE OF

The Right Hon. Viscount Hampden,

AT

GLYNDE, SUSSEX.

PRINTED AT THE "SUSSEX ADVERTISER" OFFICE, LEWES.

The front page of the official programme for the opening of the Telpher Line.

way trucks parked on the railway siding. After inspecting the Tramway works the party retired to the Trevor Arms where a luncheon was provided. The usual series of speeches were given wishing great success to the venture. No doubt The Telpherage Company Limited ensured that the ceremony was given coverage in newspapers,

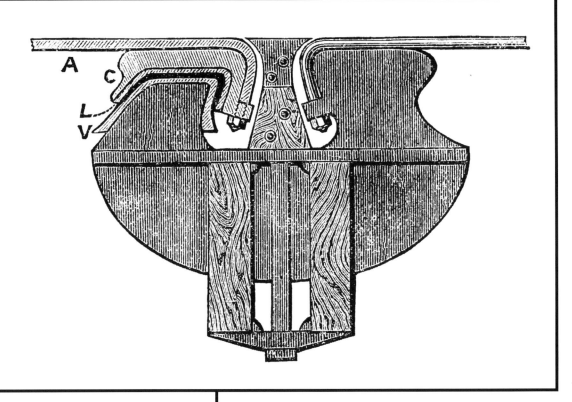

Above: The supports for the running rods (that are the electrical supply) also act as insulators.

both local and further afield and technical magazines.

However, it was largely ignored. This was demonstrated in an article in the Pall Mall Gazette of 31st January 1888 when the reporter was surprised to find the Telpherage system operating and that it had not attracted more attention. The Glynde system had been operating for two years, but had attracted little publicity. The article did describe the operation as using 'trams' of ten skeps each set ten feet apart and connected by light rods. Each skep carried 3cwt of clay, giving a total load of one ton and its motor could be disconnected using a switch attached to the motor. The weight of the trams would distort the wire rails into a catenary shape, but the length of the tram train was such that the skeps going uphill were counterbalanced by skeps going downhill. The speed of the locomotives was regulated automatically giving a consistent speed of travel. The line cost £1,200 and was equipped with five trams able to carry a total of 100 tons of clay each day and 360 tons of clay every week, making considerable savings over taking the clay by horse and cart. There was an unexpected side effect of the Tramway. Passengers on the railway to Eastbourne that ran alongside the Tramway had a grand view of the line that attracted considerable attention.

The Glynde Aerial Tramway was built as a purely mineral line for transporting clay. However, workmen would have ridden in the trucks for maintenance and repair purposes. They were able to stop at any point, to inspect or effect repairs, by the sim-

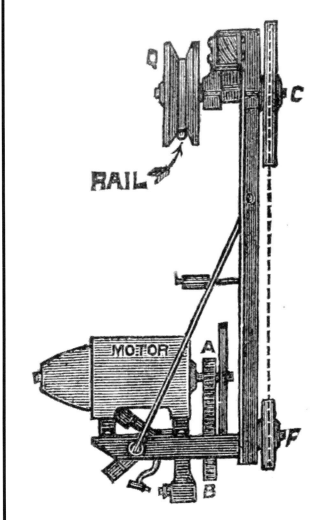

The motor and drive of the power unit on the centre car of each tram. As it always ran in the same direction if the polarity was reversed, there was a switch to enable the unit to run in reverse.

ple process of using an on-off switch on the locomotive. Given the nature of the ground (much was swampy) it went across, no doubt other workmen would have taken informal rides in order to get from one end of the line to the other. The manufacturers did indicate that the system could be used for passenger transport, by replacing the bucket with a seat that could hold two people. But there is no record of this being used on the Glynde Telpher.

At its Annual Meeting in February 1888 the Chairman of the Sussex Portland Cement Company commented that the Company had recently purchased the Tramway. It had proved to be an extremely cheap carrier to the Company. The cost to the Company was £250 deposit and £150 further if the line proved satisfactory. It had cost The Telpherage Company Limited over £3,000, who expressed pleasure over the advantageous terms. The Chairman also commented that further savings would be made by extending the line right to the pits. However, it seems that the optimism was somewhat misplaced as the Company applied on 13th July 1889 for permission to replace the Telpher line with a tramway. It is believed that demand for the clay increased and the line could not meet the increased loads. The new Tramway required a bridge over

Glynde Reach at the same place where the Telpher bridge was. It was also proposed to operate the line using horses or steam engines. The Company urged the authority to give a prompt response as the Telpher system had been giving trouble. Indeed, a newspaper report in September 1889 stated that the Telpher system had stopped running. A later statement from the Telpher Company insisted that the Telpher was working and that the short stop had been temporary. However, it seems that the Telpher was not satisfactory as at the Annual Meeting of the Cement Company in October 1890 the Chairman reported that a conventional tramway had replaced the Telpher line.

FLEET

There were five trams each consisting of ten skeps and one central power unit. There is no record of the use of any numbering system.

LIVERY

Black, white and light brown.

The drawings that were made during the life of the railway differ significantly in detail, so should be taken as broad representations rather then precise reproductions of the actual Tramway.

CHAPTER 11

DEVIL'S DYKE AERIAL TRAMWAY 1894 - 1909

A view of the whole of the Aerial Tramway. The carriage has just left the nearest station. It appears there is another carriage at the midpoint. In fact the Tramway only ever had one carriage.

The Devil's Dyke, situated five miles from Brighton on the South Downs, has been a popular spot to visit from early times. To cater for the tourists, local people converted their wagonettes to passenger carts by adding small wooden chairs. The standard fare charged was 1/6d that rose to 2/-d on special days. The journey took an hour each way, with an hour spent at the beauty spot. A hotel was built in 1831 to serve the holiday makers. This was rebuilt in 1871 and was a popular attraction. Local entrepreneurs proposed building a railway to the Dyke, making it far easier for holiday makers. The plans were to build it as a branch off the LBSC Brighton to Worthing line and a Bill was presented to Parliament in 1873, but was withdrawn. Another attempt was made in 1874, but disagreements between the railway Company and the land owners, the Marquis of Abergavenny and Lord Leconfield meant it too was withdrawn. A third attempt to gain authorisation for the line came in 1877 and this was successful. A new Company The Brighton and Dyke Railway Company was incorporated to build and run the railway. The Company had £72,000 capital, however, it was slow in building the line and in 1881 had to seek extensions to the Act. The line was formally

opened on 1st September 1887. It was an immediate success with extra trains having to be put on during the first Sundays. However, once the initial enthusiasm abated, the passenger numbers were lower than had been anticipated.

Despite the initial disappointment of the Railway Company, the numbers of visitors to the area increased considerably and using the railway meant that they could stay far longer than the hour allowed by the wagonettes. William Brewer, an American Civil Engineer, proposed three additional entertainments around the Dyke. The first was a cable Tramway to provide a public transport link between the Dyke Railway Station and the Dyke Estate. The second was an entertaining ride called the aerial Tramway across the gorge and finally another fairground type ride, the steep grade Tramway up the steep section of the Dyke. Nothing came of the cable Tramway, but the aerial Tramway and steep grade Tramway were built. Below is a description of the aerial Tramway and the next section of the book examines the Steep Grade Tramway.

The idea behind the aerial Tramway (the ride was

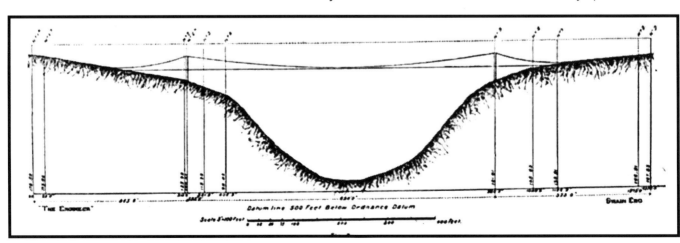

Profile of the Dyke where the Aerial Tramway crosses it.

The passenger tram with the Attendant standing at the rear. The ride must have been both exciting and frightening for the passengers.

worthy people, both political and professional, were invited to the formal opening. The Mayor of Brighton performed the opening ceremony and then, with the Mayoress, Mr W. Brewer; and Mr W. T. Spink, the Chairman of the Telpher Company, they boarded the car and travelled over the Dyke and back. The Mayor proclaimed the journey to be "heavenly". Afterwards the party and guests retired to the Pavilion on the Dyke Estate for lunch and the obligatory speeches. Following the proceedings, the party returned to the Tramway to enjoy another journey.

given a number of names including aerial cableway, but I have chosen to use the term tramway) was to provide an exciting trip high above the Dyke, from one side to the other. Mr Brewer, with Mr Scott-Russell and Mr Lothian, established the Telpher Cable and Cliff Railway Syndicate, Limited in 1893 to promote the building of the ride. Capital was raised, using a working model of the proposed structure. Some £5,000 capital was required and this was found (mainly from a Mr J. H. Hubbard, owner of the Dyke Hotel), enabling the project to go ahead. The Cable Tramways Construction and Conversion Company Limited was contracted to build the aerial Tramway. It was completed and formally opened on 13th October 1894.

The structure consisted of two towers, one each side of the Dyke, with cables hung between them. These supported the track cables making it look very much like a suspension bridge. The distance between the towers was 650ft, while the total length of the structure was 1,200ft There were stations at each end to enable passengers to board and alight from the car. The fare for a single journey in either direction was 6d. The passenger car was hauled by an endless cable that was powered by a Crossley internal combustion engine located near the north station. There was one passenger car that had open sides (no health and safety in those days) to allow maximum visibility for the four seated passengers. An attendant stood at one end of the car. The maximum height above the ground was 230ft. The journey time from one station to the other was 2¼ minutes. An unusual aspect of the design was that the car travelled through the support columns.

As was usual in those days, a large number of

It was not unexpected that some people criticised the Tramway as "desecrating the beauty spot". The local newspaper "Devil's Dyke Times", on the other hand, was in favour describing the Tramway with "the delight of a trip on this railway can only be experienced, it is too delicious to be described". The Tramway was an immediate success with hundreds of visitors travelling on it. However, like many novelties the initial enthusiasm gradually wore off. The number of passengers gradually declined and the enterprise began losing money. Such were the business problems encountered by Mr Hubbard, the main shareholder, that he emigrated to Toronto, Canada in 1907. The Tramway was in difficulties, though managed to continue for a couple of years. But around 1909 the enterprise closed. The final indignity occurred in 1914 when it was used as target practice by First World War troops, who succeeded in demolishing it.

FLEET

A single passenger carriage.

LIVERY

Not known

A view across the Dyke with the carriage nearing the halfway point.

CHAPTER 12

DEVIL'S DYKE STEEP GRADE TRAMWAY 1897 - 1908

The upper station of the Steep Grade Tramway with one of the two cars about to enter the platform.

Called at the time a steep grade Tramway, it would today be described as a funicular. The promotor was Mr J. H. Hubbard, who also funded the aerial Tramway. Both projects were aimed at increasing visitor numbers to the Devil's Dyke and thus promoting trade at the Dyke Hotel, owned by Mr Hubbard. The steep grade Tramway actually ran on the slope north of the Dyke itself. Starting close to the hotel it ran down the gradient to terminate within a short walk from Poynings Village. The concept was that visitors from Brighton would travel by horse brake to the hotel or by railway to Dyke Station, walk the short distance to the hotel, then travel down the steep grade Tramway and walk to the village of Poynings where they could enjoy "Sussex Teas" before making the return journey.

Like many Victorian enterprises the organisational structure was complex. Mr Hubbard owned the land around the hotel, including the proposed track bed of the steep grade railway. He agreed to grant a lease (at £100 per annum) to the Pyramidical Syndicate Ltd, based in London, for the land the railway required by his hotel. Another Company, the Brighton Dyke Steep Grade Railway was established in 1896 with the aim of owning and operating the railway. Also the Railway Company was to pay the Pyramidical Company £9,000. The Railway Company issued 10,000 shares at £1 to acquire the neces-

sary capital. The £9,000 was to come from the £10,000 accumulated from selling the shares.

Construction began in 1896 for a 3ft gauge double track line. The line itself was unusual for a funicular as it had three different gradients. The top section was built with a 1:1.8 gradient, while the central section was steeper with a gradient of 1:1.5 and finally the lowest section was more gentle with a 1:2.9 gradient. The whole line was 840ft long (an advertisement for the hotel claimed the line was 876ft long)

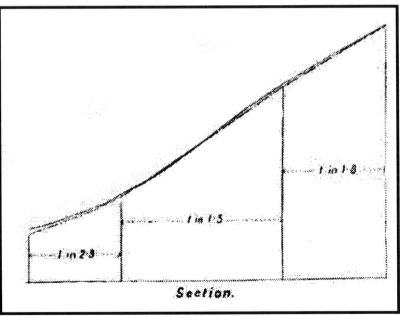

Cross section of the line showing the changes in gradient demanded by the terrain.

with a gain in height of 395ft. Power came from a Hornsby-Ackroyd internal combustion engine mounted at the top of the funicular. It was housed in the top station building. There was a platform but no building at the bottom of the funicular. The line operated in the usual funicular manner, the two cars being linked by cable, one going up as the other descended. Each car had a capacity of 14 passengers. The cars had roofs, but the sides were open. The fare was 2d each way. Mr Hubbard also planned to use the line to transport goods and farm produce to his hotel.

Charles Blaber was Engineer for the steep grade railway (he was also Engineer for the Dyke Railway). The railway was constructed by Messrs Courtney & Birkett of Southwick, strangely a local shipbuilder. It was formally opened on 24th July 1897 by Sir Henry Howarth MP. He made a short speech at the station at the top of the funicular. Then the party travelled in the cars, admiring the scenery. When all were back at the top, they walked to the hotel for luncheon, with many speeches and toasts.

It proved to be a great success with the public. At the next Bank Holiday, the line was so popular that it was taking

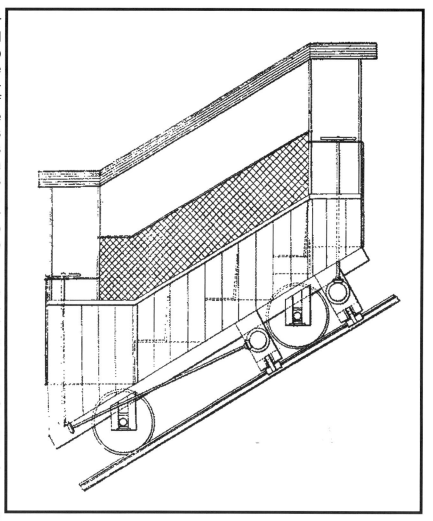

One of the two carriages used on the Tramway.

£5 an hour in receipts. However, there was a unforeseen consequence. Visitors would arrive by train and go directly to the Steep Grade Railway without bothering to enter the hotel. A similar situation happened on their return journeys. To Mr Hubbard's disappointment takings at the hotel actually fell. Rather like the aerial Tramway, the funicular rather quickly fell out of favour. By 1899 it had ceased running. In addition, Court action was taken against the railway to reveal its financial situation. It was found that the Company owed £4,766 5s 6d to the Pyramidical Syndicate Ltd. The shareholders realised that they were likely to lose all the investments. The only way to recoup

Looking up the whole of the line. Note the lack of facilities at the bottom.

some of their money was to purchase the railway cheaply as a non-running, bankrupt concern and to re-open it. The railway was sold by auction on 13th December 1900. The shareholders managed to purchase it for £390. They began operating it, but it was no longer the attraction it used to be. A motor bus route had been established taking visitors to Poynings by road. To compound the problems, the hotel was attracting day trippers who did not want to travel on the funicular. The result was an inevitable decline and it closed in 1908 with the equipment being removed in 1913.

FLEET

Two funicular cars, there is no record them being numbered.

LIVERY

Not known

The whole funicular with the two cars passing at the mid-point. Note the complete lack of facilities at the bottom end.

The upper station of the Steep Grade Tramway with one of the cars approaching the terminus.

CHAPTER 13

PALACE PIER TRAMWAY 1899 - 1901

An early photograph of Palace Pier nearing completion. In order to generate revenue the pier was opened before being finished. Construction of the concert hall can be seen at the end of the pier. Unfortunately the Tramway rails are not visible. *Author's collection.*

In 2001 the Palace Pier in Brighton was renamed "Brighton Pier", but this history will keep to the original name, as that was the one in use at the time it had a Tramway. It was one of three piers built in Brighton. The first was the Chain Pier, opened in 1823 that was built to serve the cross Channel ferries. However, in 1847 a deep water port was opened at Newhaven and the pier became redundant and it was closed in 1896 after a violent storm washed much of it away. The second pier to open was the West Pier in 1866 and was a public attraction. However, in the 1970s seaside holidays were unfashionable and the limited number of visitors meant the pier was a financial burden to its owners. Indeed, the owning Company went into liquidation and the pier closed. Various attempts were made to rebuild and reopen it, but all came to nought. Then in 2002/3 storms significantly damaged the pier, and part of it fell into the sea. Then later in 2003 it was subject to two arson attacks which further damaged the structure, much of which appears derelict with the central structure having collapsed. Currently there seem to be no plans to do anything other than let it rot away.

The final pier to be built was the Palace Pier (originally called the Brighton Marine Palace). Designed by Richard St George Moore, building started in November 1881, but construction took longer than planned. The work was not helped by a severe storm in 1896 that damaged the Chain Pier, parts of which were washed into the Palace Pier. The owners, the Marine Palace and Pier Company, decided to call it a day and liquidated the Company. Howev-

er, Sir James Howard stepped in with an offer of financial help and work went ahead. It took another three years of construction before it could be opened on the 20th May 1899, despite not being finished. The admission to the 1760 feet long pier was 2d, which gave access to the Dining Room, Grill Room, Smoking and Reading Rooms and a bathing platform. Having opened it, the Company continued building as they wanted to add a Pavilion and Winter Garden at the end of the pier. To assist in the building work a tramway track was laid along the centre of the pier in 1899. This was used to convey building materials and a truck was propelled by hand. This was purely a goods operation, but no doubt some of the workers took advantage of it to get a free ride along the length of the pier. Once the construction work was completed the Tramway was no longer required and the rails were lifted. Unfortunately, no photographs of the track or the wagon have been found.

FLEET

Unknown number of unpowered wagons.

LIVERY

Not known.

CHAPTER 14

SEAFRONT MONORAIL 2009 TO DATE

An artist's impression of the proposed sea front monorail. *Photograph Paris-Normandie.*

The first hint at building a monorail along the Brighton coast came in 1968 when the Brighton and Hove Herald carried a fictionional article by the Junior Chamber of Commerce where King Charles III opened a sea front monorail in the town. It was envisaged that up to 1,200 people an hour could be taken to Shoreham on a ten minute journey.

The idea was taken up in 2001 with the incorporation of the Brighton Monorail Company Limited on 2nd April. Little was heard of the Company and in 2002 the Company name was changed on 20th September 2002 to the Brighton Monorail and Tram Company Limited. There was another name change on 2nd April 2008 when it reverted back to the Brighton Monorail Company Limited. In June 2009 the people behind the Company, local businessmen David Courtney and John Reagan met with Mary Mears, the Conservative leader of Brighton and Hove City Council, to discuss their proposals to build a monorail along the seafront from Palace Pier to the Marina. Local newspaper, The Brighton Argos, reported that Councillor Mears told other Councillors: "We are very keen to look at all forms of transport. There is a work in progress on the monorail and as soon as it's a firmer proposal it will be coming to Committee. It's quite exciting. It's another form of transport and an advert for the city." Councillor Gill Mitchell, Labour opposition leader, said the monorail was not a serious transport scheme. Original plans for the monorail had been rejected by Labour, when they ran the Council, in favour of a bus-based rapid transport scheme (RTS) that would be cheaper to maintain and build and offer greater flexibility. He added that it would mean there would be three traffic schemes: the road, the Volks Railway and then the monorail. It would form a huge boundary between Kemp Town and the beach. Councillor Mears said that the RTS and a park and ride scheme would be looked at again and that if successful the monorail would be extended to Shoreham Harbour.

The newspaper added the report to its website and people were able to comment on the proposal. There were 24 responses and all were against the idea. There was no one who gave any support at all to the scheme. The main objections were that it was unnecessary, would obstruct the views and access to the beach, cost a large sum of money and would have little use. Nothing further was heard from the Brighton Monorail Company Limited and the Company was dissolved on 14th January 2014.

However, this was not the last to be heard of a monorail. The issue was raised by Nick Lomax in 2016 as part of an overall plan to redevelop the seafront. His plans, that were described in the Brighton Journal for 13th January, were wide ranging and included splitting the seafront into seven zones; rebuilding the West Pier as a double deck construction; building an art gallery; a car museum, an outdoor swimming pool and the monorail. He told The Argus "These were all just ideas and at an early stage. But they are about starting a debate on the seafront. We need to start thinking big. It was easy to say monorails and new art galleries are all pie in the sky. But other cities around the world are building these

things so why shouldn't we? If your starting point is 'well that is never going to happen anyway' then you are never going to get anywhere". The proposal included financial support for Volk's Railway with restoration funding and the construction of a new station and visitors' centre.

This prompted David Courtney to renew his efforts to promote the monorail. He admitted that they were trying not to use the word monorail as some people felt it was a bit of an old expression. Instead the project was renamed a "seafront rapid transport system". Now the proposed route was along the coast between the city's marina and Shoreham Airport. Mr Courtney is friends with Brighton-based architect Nick Lomax who had revealed his own plans the previous month - which included relocating Volk's Railway from its site in Madeira Drive. However, officials did not share the duo's enthusiasm for the scheme. This proposal also met with opposition from local residents. In response Mr Courtney accepted that not everyone was behind the ideas and he was keen on a referendum as a means of letting the people decide. To date there has been no referendum nor any sign of any move to obtain authority to start building the monorail.

FLEET

Proposal only, not built.

LIVERY

Not decided.

In 1933 the Mayor of Brighton drove Volk's Railway car 5 beside Magnus Volk to celebrate the 50th anniversary of the opening of the line.

SOURCES

Brighton District Tramways.
Brighton and District Tramways Company Ltd.
Brighton and Shoreham Tramways Company Ltd.
British Electric Traction – Brighton and Shoreham Tramways Company Ltd.

A History of Light Rail Transport in the Brighton Area of Sussex, by Ronald M. Harmer, Tramway Review, Nos 42 – 47 inclusive 1965/6.
Tramways Remembered South & South East England, Leslie Oppitz, Countryside Books, 1988.
Brighton's Tramways, Robert J. Harley, Middleton Press, 1992.
The Directory of British Tramways, by Keith Turner, pub. Patrick Stephens Ltd., 1996.
The Age of the Horse Tram, by David Voice, pub. Adam Gordon, 2000.
Tramways of the South Coast, by J. C. Gillham and R. J. S. Wiseman, pub. Light Rail Transit Association, 2004.
A History of the British Steam Tram Volume 2, by David Gladwin, pub. Adam Gordon, 2006.
Brighton and Shoreham Tramways, Wikipeadia

Brighton Corporation Tramways
Brighton Tramcar 53

Electric Traction: A Review of its Application and a Comparison with Other Methods, Proceedings of the Incorporated Association of Municipal and County Engineers, Vol XXII, 1895-96
Brighton Corporation Tramways, The Tramway and Railway World, 12th December 1901.
Inquiry into Brighton Corporation Tramways, Journal of the Municipal Tramways Association, 1922.
Brighton Corporation Tramways, The Electric Railway and Tramway Journal, 7th August 1925.
The Times Law Reports, 11th July 1930.
Proposal to Establish a Novel Transport Board, Journal of the Municipal Tramways and Transport Association, 1930.
Transport World, 14th May 1936
Centenary Exhibition and Official Programme 1854 – 1954, pub. County Borough of Brighton, 1954.
Strangers in the Camp, Surprising Changes in the Brighton Scene, Passenger Transport, 1962.
A History of Light Rail Transport in the Brighton Area of Sussex, by Ronald M. Harmer, Tramway Review, Nos 42 – 47 inclusive 1965/6.
Brighton Corporation Transport Feet History 4th Edition, R. Knight, pub. E.L.P.G. Enterprises, 1971.
Rip Van Winkle, by Fran L. Dix, pub. Tramway Review, No 94, 1978.
A Portrait of the Brighton Trams 1901 - 1939, by A. G. Elliott, pub. Author, 1979.
Serving the Community of Brighton, 85th Anniversary, by Alan J. Piatt, pub Brighton Corporation, 1986.
A Portrait of Brighton in Tram Days, by A. G. Elliott, pub. Author, 1986.
Tramways Remembered South & South East England, Leslie Oppitz, Countryside Books, 1988.
Brighton's Tramways, Robert J. Harley, Middleton Press, 1992.
The Directory of British Tramways, by Keith Turner, pub. Patrick Stephens Ltd., 1996.
Circular Tour, Seaside Pleasure Riding by Tram, by Brian Turner, pub. Rio Vista, 1999.
The Tickets of the Brighton Corporation Tramways, by Rev. P. S.G. Lidgett, pub. Omnibus Society, 2001.
Depot Watch 7, Brighton Sussex, by N. A. Kellet, pub. Tramway Review, No 185, 2001.
From Tramshed to Go-Ahead, by Peter Ticehurst and Alan Piatt, 2002
Tramways of the South Coast, by J. C. Gillham and R. J. S. Wiseman, pub. Light Rail Transit Association, 2004.
The Argus, 9th April 2014
https://www.brightontram53.org.uk
https://www.facebook.com/Brightontram53society/
https://btontram53.blogspot.com

Parry People Mover

The Green Line, Progress Report on the Development of a Revolutionary Flywheel-Powered Light Rail System, pub Parry People Movers, c1993.
The Parry People Mover Introducing an Affordable Light Tramway System, pub Parry People Movers, c1994.
http://www.photosbrightonandhove.org.uk/portfolio/transport/parry-people-mover-on-trial.html
http://www.luxury-yacht.co.uk/parrypeoplemover.htm
http://www.mybrightonandhove.org.uk/page/trams_and_trolley_buses-2

Volk's Electric Railway
Brighton and Rottingdean Seashore Electric Tramway

Electric Traction: A Review of its Application and a Comparison with Other Methods, Proceedings of the Incorporated Association of Municipal and County Engineers, Vol XXII, 1895-96
A Novel Seashore Electric Tramway, by Magnus Volk, Cassiers Magazine, July 1896.
Volk's Electric Railway and How it is Worked, by Magnus Volk, pub. Author, c1899.
Volk's Railway Brighton, 1883 – 1964, by Alan A. Jackson, pub. Light Railway Transport League, 1964
A History of Light Rail Transport in the Brighton Area of Sussex, by Ronald M. Harmer, Tramway Review, Nos 42 – 47 inclusive 1965/6.
Magnus Volk of Brighton, by Comrad Volk, pub. Phillimore & Co. Ltd.,1971.
Volk's Railway Brighton, by Alan A. Jackson, pub. Light Railway Transport League, c1972.
Volk's Railway Brighton 1883 – 1983 Centenary, by Jenny Pulling, pub. Brighton Borough Council, 1983.
Tramways Remembered South & South East England, Leslie Oppitz, Countryside Books, 1988.
Brighton's Tramways, Robert J. Harley, Middleton Press, 1992.
Volk's Railway Brighton, An Illustrated History, by Alan A. Jackson, pub. Plateway Press, 1993.
The Directory of British Tramways, by Keith Turner, pub. Patrick Stephens Ltd., 1996.
Tramways of the South Coast, by J. C. Gillham and R. J. S. Wiseman, pub. Light Rail Transit Association, 2004.
A Tale of Many Railways – An Autobiography & History of Alan Keef Ltd., by Alan Keef, pub Lightmoor Press, 2008
Magnus Volk's Electric Railway – A Pictorial History 1883 – 2010, by Derek Smith, pub. Author, 2010.
Magnus Volk's Electric Railway – A Pictorial History 1883 – 2016, by Derek Smith, pub. Author, 2017.
'The Example Which We Have Seized Upon': Magnus Volk's Electric Railways, by Geoffrey Skelsey, Tramway Review No 258 June 2019
Volk's Railway: More Information, by Ian Gledhill, Tramway Review No 259 September 2019
https://www.volksrailway.org.uk
https://en-gb.facebook.com/VolksElectricRailwayAssociation

Glynde Aerial Tramway
Devil's Dyke Aerial Tramway
Devil's Dyke Steep Grade Tramway

York Herald, 23rd April 1885.
Pall Mall Gazette, 31st January 1888.
Sussex Express, 11th February 1888, 16th July 1889, 25th October 1890, 11th February 1891
West Briton and Cornwall Advertiser, 12th September 1889
Telpherage in Practical Use, by Frederik Atherton Fernald Popular Science Monthly, July 1890
Sussex Express, 25th Oct 1890
The Glynde Archivist, number 2, 1985
Mineral Transport by the Telpher System – The Pioneering Work of Prof H. C. F. Fleeming-Jenkin (the Story of the Glynde Aerial Railway), by M. I. Pope, pub. Sussex Industrial History No 17, 1987.
A History of Glynde, www.glynde.info/history/
www.urban75.org/railway/devils-dyke.html
http://fulking.net/the-aerial-cableway-1894-1909/
http://www.urban75.org/railway/devils-dyke.html
http://www.hows.org.uk/personal/rail/dd.htm

Palace Pier Tramway

Illustrated London News, 27th May 1899.
Walking Over the Waves, Quintessential British Seaside Piers, by Chris Foote Wood, pub. Whittles Publishing, 2016.
Brighton Palace Pier, Wikipedia.
https://piers.org.uk/pier/brighton-palace/

Seafront Monorail

The Argos, 13th June 2009.23rd
Brighton Journal, 13th January 2016.
http://brightoniana.com/brighton-and-hove-as-it-might-have-been/why-brightons-seafront-monorail-failed-to-fly/